Praise for *The Defiant Middle*

"This is a wonderful, wonderful book. While excavating and illuminating the everyday and profound in-betweens that women traverse, it is also an insightful meditation on the liminal realities of religion, and of life writ large. And it is so beautifully, winsomely written! I plan to give this book to every woman I know, beginning with my mother and my daughter."

—Krista Tippett, founder and CEO of the On Being Project

"*The Defiant Middle* is the book I didn't know I needed to read. Writing as both companion and guide, Oakes brings readers into conversation with women who have come before, with women who have refused to conform to the categories and expectations imposed upon them. The result is an enlightening rumination on spirituality and embodiment, on the constraints women face, and also the possibilities available to women as they navigate their own journeys."

—Kristin Kobes Du Mez, author of *Jesus and John Wayne*

"*The Defiant Middle* is a life-giving book bound to stir up more questions than give definitive answers. Like the women she admires and wonders about, Kaya Oakes is a guide and companion to the parts of female life and spirituality that are neglected, dismissed, erased, and ignored. For anyone who has ever felt too much of anything, they are bound to feel both seen and known in these pages—and learn to wonder quite a bit at all the complicated stories we have flattened in our history and theology books. Kaya Oakes continues to stand out as one of the best essayists of our time, bringing both her Catholic and gen-x imagination into these thoughtful, complicated pages"

—D. L. Mayfield, author of *The Myth of the American Dream: Reflections on Affluence, Autonomy, Safety, and Power*

"This book is vulnerable and real. For those of us who live in the liminal space known as middle age, *The Defiant Middle* will change and challenge how we navigate this stage of life. With wit and clarity, Kaya Oakes invites you to reconsider and reevaluate what you think you know by offering her own brilliant insights and the tested wisdom of the saints who've gone before us. In a world of polarities, Oakes speaks to the women in the middle with nuance and dimension. This is a book that will sit by my bedside because it's filled with words I don't want to forget."

—Karen González, author of *The God Who Sees:
Immigrants, the Bible, and the Journey to Belong*

"With razor-sharp wit Kaya Oakes cuts to ribbons the last shreds of patriarchy and makes more room for all women to inhabit the spiritual, religious, relational, political, and prophetic selves God has ordained, in defiance of expectations. *The Defiant Middle* will delight and liberate people of any gender who are ready for its composite wisdom."

—Molly Baskette, senior minister,
First Church Berkley, UCC

THE
DEFIANT
MIDDLE

HOW WOMEN CLAIM LIFE'S
IN-BETWEENS TO REMAKE THE WORLD

KAYA OAKES

Broadleaf Books
Minneapolis

THE DEFIANT MIDDLE
How Women Claim Life's In-Betweens to Remake the World

Cover design and illustration: James Kegley

Print ISBN: 978-1-5064-6768-9
eBook ISBN: 978-1-5064-6769-6

In memory of Paula and Kathleen, and for my nieces and nephew, who will remake the world.

Women in time will come to do much.
　　　　　　　　　　　　—MARY WARD, 1585–1645

CONTENTS

PRELUDE
The Middle, the Medieval, and the In-Between

It starts happening before you realize it, and by the time you do, the slow, grinding erasures have already begun. At church, the young adult group gets mentioned repeatedly, and even though you look around and realize you're still one of the youngest people there, you've crossed the mysterious river into no longer being a young adult. You're also very frequently alone in church. Your own generation, the one that was Xed out before it found an identity, lost interest in Christianity around the time of Reagan's "shining city on a hill" and Tammy Faye Bakker's smeared mascara, and only one of your fellow born-in-the-seventies friends takes her faith very seriously, and she's a priest, so it's her job. Yet here you are, still trying.

You're too young for the "Senior Celebration of Life!" at church but too old for the "baseball and beer" excursion with a firmly underlined reminder that "anyone <u>under 40</u> is welcome." You're too old to be on social media but too young to quit. The wrong shape for those jeans but still somehow the wrong shape for those other jeans.

Too bland to have so many tattoos but too interesting to stop getting them. Too ambitious to settle for an easy life but too self-critical to settle into anything for long. Too angry, too crazy, too predictable, too surprising, too smart, too capable. You're a woman, so you are always too much.

A younger friend says you look "good for your age," but you're not sure what that means when you watch *Big Little Lies* and realize Nicole Kidman, four years your senior, has perfectly undisturbed, luminescent skin, like the shimmering surface of a faraway planet, while your own face is forked and pitted. You look for other TV shows, movies, or books about women like you, women who are neither old nor young, neither fat nor thin, neither pretty nor ugly, neither this nor that, and in each of them, the woman is screaming, crying, throwing her phone, frowning in a dressing room, getting divorced, getting cancer, fighting with her children, fighting with her parents, or embarrassing herself repeatedly, every single day. She is, in a word, messy.

But what exactly do we expect a woman to be? In the Roman Catholic tradition, which is the religious and intellectual lens through which I was taught to see the world, the image of Mary as a meek, mild, blonde, and white model of female perfection has caused centuries of problems for the vast majority of women who are nothing like that, including Mary herself. The real Mary, a revolutionarily minded Jewish woman who grew up under the rule of an empire, does not resemble the plaster statues that watched over me in my own girlhood. But I did not meet that Mary until I was well into adulthood. Nor did I meet Dorothy Day, Mary Magdalene, Sister Thea Bowman, Pauli Murray, Julian of Norwich, Dolores Huerta, or any other potential religious role model who resisted those narrow definitions of Christian womanhood—until decades after I graduated from Catholic school.

The notions about what women should do, think, and feel are entrenched in religion, culture, and history and remain stubbornly persistent well into this fourth wave of feminism. We're expected to be both nurturing and independent. Angry and tranquil. "One of the boys" and still femme enough to be sexually viable. Racism and classism have made the aspirational image of a thin, wealthy white woman normative, when it is far from realistic for the vast majority. Women are expected to be fertile (otherwise your body is dismissed as a barren wasteland), but not too fertile (otherwise you're burdening society). Self-sacrificing, but not selfless. Women can cry picturesquely on occasion, but clinical depression and anxiety have to be brushed aside or sublimated, because we are always expected to be doing something for someone. We should love and accept our imperfect bodies but still not gain weight or "let ourselves go." We should have a "girl squad" and we should never go anywhere without them, rather than preferring, at least on occasion, to be alone. We can be smart but not brilliant, impressive but not intimidating, friendly but not fawning.

To fail to live up to these expectations can be a declaration of defiance, of resistance to categorization and pushing back against expectations. These kinds of women are also messy, because they're agents of change, and change is messy. And yet, like every other woman, they're still expected to clean up the mess.

Five years ago, I sat across from my spiritual director, rattling off this same series of complaints. I felt messy, every day. He asked exactly how old I was. When I said I'd just turned forty-five, he sighed. "That's a hard age," he told me. Something shifted. I'd been rolling the Sisyphean boulder of my age for years, just waiting for things to get easier, as other women kept reassuring me they would. Apparently, at some time, I would reach a magical point when I had "no fucks left to give." But no one had warned me that before I hit that magical point, I'd have to survive something harder: the in-between years, which never seemed to end.

And, in fact, I still had many fucks left to give.

Numerically, I am today middle-aged, somewhere between young and old. But I resist the term *middle-aged*, not because of its unfriendly reminder that I've hit some Dante-esque pivot point at which I've become lost in a dark wood, but because I don't know what I'm in the middle of. And how can any of us know we are in the middle when the end is unclear?

To find a location, I wondered, What if, instead of being caught in between expectations and reality, we thought of ourselves as medieval? It was in that era when many women also defied expectations and reinvented themselves, along with their world.

The medieval imagination was often male. The dark wood where Dante is lost is the *selva oscura*: in the medieval imagination, it was a place where questing knights became lost and disoriented among the trees, their paths forward put on hold while they went mad due to a loss of direction. These knights, however, were always men. Men were expected to explore and wander. For them, it was a noble cause.

Women, on the other hand, had little agency, almost no control over their bodies, and brutally short lives. When they entered the *selva oscura* there was a very different cultural response—and cost. But there were always exceptions, in that era and others, and those exceptions can help us understand that being caught between expectations placed on the women themselves and the reality of the time can be spiritually and creatively fruitful, even if that often comes with sacrifice.

Hildegard von Bingen, Julian of Norwich, Joan of Arc, Margery Kempe, and other women in the medieval era were all examples of defiance against what women were expected to be because of their culture, gender, and religion. And this defiant streak would appear again and again in women across the centuries, manifesting in many different ways and shifting our ways of understanding the world.

At the age of forty-three, Hildegard (who had been having mystical religious visions since she was three) wrote, "I heard a voice from Heaven saying to me, 'Cry out therefore, and write thus.'"[1]

As she moved into her fifties and sixties, Hildegard's fevered imagination couldn't be held in by the confines of Latin, the language of the church, so she invented her own alphabet, the *Lingua Ignota*, or "unknown language."

She also wrote about medicine and even served as a pharmacist for her community. She wrote sixty-nine musical compositions, along with the largest surviving collection of letters from the medieval era. And in a time when many women were confined to the home or to cloistered monasteries—and within the boundaries of the Catholic church, which is still closed to the ordination of women today—Hildegard embarked on preaching tours throughout Germany, calling out clerical corruption.

The kind of subversion Hildegard modeled was echoed in the lives of other women throughout the medieval era. Roughly a hundred years later, the British mystic Julian of Norwich also pushed the boundaries of our understanding of God. The first woman to write a book in English, the language of the people rather than of the church hierarchy, Julian referred to Christ as both mother and brother, unbound by gender but capable of boundless compassion. In the *Revelations*, she gives us a creed most useful to women trapped between expectations and reality: "Thou shalt not be overcome."[2]

Medieval women can be mentors to us in the in-between. In an era when women were so often held back or silenced, their brazenness and creativity made them models of agency and self-identity. Hildegard, Julian, and other medieval women like Joan of Arc stood up to church authorities by creating forms of life for their religious communities, putting their visions into words, and sometimes putting their bodies on the line for the sake of what they believed.

Today, we often take feminism and what it's given us for granted, which makes it harder to understand how unusual these women were in the context of their time—and the cost of their choices and work. Medieval women were censored, silenced, accused of heresy, and sometimes killed for what they said and wrote. But what they and other women throughout history who stood in between expectations and reality offer us today is a different way of thinking. What was pushed to the margins, cloistered, and silenced feels absolutely contemporary. The end of the medieval era, after all, was the beginning of the Renaissance.

Today, women are still hemmed in by expectations of what we should be, but we are also coming to new understandings about age, youth, anger, mental health, the meaning of fertility, solitude, and independence. When women feel the freedom to evolve beyond prescribed roles, we can experience a fecundity of the imagination, an era when we become not solely creative, but creation.

It is not just the medieval era that offers us examples of women who have used the spaces between expectations and reality for reinvention. The seed of this book was planted in the stories of medieval women, but as it grew, it stretched into other eras, moved through religion and into literature and entertainment and medicine and

politics because women in every field are always expected
to be so many things to so many people. In every era.

In my reading and research, I kept returning to those
women who were too old, too young, too barren, too
butch/femme/other, too crazy, too angry, too alone. They
were both in between and on the edges. Many more categories of *too other* could be added, and clearly, many of
these expectations of women are placed on them by men.
Toxic masculinity—the way "traditional" ideas of manhood
have turned on themselves and curdled into a violent,
self-loathing, woman-hating stew—is part of the reason
women and men alike are so caged in by gender "ideals."

In some ways, we are in the same boat, but women
are doing most of the rowing while men are still steer-
ing the ship. This is part of why any investigation of
what we expect from women means we also have to
ask what we expect to gain from cleaving to an increasingly useless and troubling focus on any static or binary
ideas of gender. "Complementarianism" has much to
answer for and has done centuries of damage we are just
beginning to undo today.

When it comes to what we expect from women, these
themes of age, attitude, caretaking, and behavior keep
repeating throughout history and remain persistent today.
Yet there are women from across history who show us
how to navigate those in-between spaces, women who
fell far short of perfection and failed to fit into prescribed
roles for the times they lived in, but who still managed to
create themselves, rather than letting social expectations

dictate their creation. As I came to know these women, I read and wrote and learned. I will always be learning from them. Perhaps all of us can.

When we live in the in-between eras, we know enough history to understand how women have been confined, and we can learn from how they defied confinement. So we, in turn, defy our own confinements and grow beyond other people's definitions of what we should be.

We reinvent ourselves and our world.

YOUNG ONE

Greta Thunberg was the hero we didn't know we needed. She went from staging a strike outside the Swedish Parliament to global celebrity for her activism to multiple Nobel prize nominations before she turned seventeen. Referring to her form of autism as her "superpower," she quickly became an icon to the neurodiverse community, to her fellow teenagers, to environmentalists, and, finally, to people of all ages watching climate change ravage the planet. Thunberg's persistence and frank, critical speeches cut through the clutter and noise of contemporary culture to people hungry for a leader in an age when global leaders were flailing.

And just a few years prior to Thunberg's arrival on a carbon-neutral ship, Malala Yousafzai became the youngest person to win a Nobel Peace Prize. Malala's activism began when she was only eleven years old, when she wrote blogs for the BBC about life under Taliban rule in Pakistan. As her activism against the ban on girls' education grew along with her public profile, the Taliban shot her in the head when she was only fifteen. Her recovery was watched by people around the world, and shortly after she was released from the hospital, a German journalist referred to her as "the most famous teenager in the world."[1]

Thunberg and Yousafzai are meeting the moment and providing new models for women who have grown up in the fourth wave of feminism, with its emphasis on intersectionality and identity at the forefront. What makes them "different"–Thunberg's position on the autism spectrum and Yousafzai's religion and ethnicity—is a large part of why they're celebrated, and the hunger for them to step into public leadership roles while they were both still in high school is unprecedented for women from my own generation, who did not see young women leading in the same ways. Add in the rising profiles of teenage gun-control activists and shooting survivors like Emma Gonzales, and sexual abuse survivors Rachael Denhollander and Chanel Miller, along with newcomer politicians like Alexandria Ocasio-Cortez and Ilhan Omar, it becomes clearer than ever that women of an emerging age are in many ways leading the conversation about the changes our world is desperately in need of.

The media often comments on these younger women by describing them as "mature," and often with a tone of surprise. While we have been aware for decades, if not hundreds or thousands of years, that girls mature faster than boys, we also have to acknowledge that the world these girls were born into may have played an out-sized part in the urgency of their activism.

Previous generations didn't see climate change accelerating as fast as it's now moving (or they chose to deny it), didn't see mass school shootings as a regular occurrence, didn't witness the courage of the #MeToo movement or the crushing defeat of a high-profile, competent woman running for president. Young women are mature not only because of their own choices, but because of the choices of the generations that came before them and the wreckage those generations left in their wake.

But the shadow side of this iconography of young women as girl warriors and child leaders is, of course, that they will grow into women subject to the same patriarchal and misogynist world as their elders. Women have changed; the attitudes of the world we live in toward women have not. And there's a danger in freezing women at a certain phase of their lives, particularly a young one. As of this writing, Malala is twenty-three, a graduate of Oxford, and well on her way to forming an adult identity. Thunberg, as young as she still looks, will graduate from high school—school strike notwithstanding—within a year of my writing this. Yet we will continue to think of them as young, long past their actually being young.

Youth, like age, is yet another liminal space women are forced into, another middle era. We are told it is good to be young but also reminded we are too young to understand things, to change them, to figure things out on our own. From the time a sixteen-year-old Joan of Arc strapped on a suit of armor and rode to meet the king of France and offer her services as a soldier, to her trial for heresy and burning at the stake three short years later, the mythical child-warrior-woman has become a common trope in religion, mythology, literature, and art. Without Joan, there's no Katniss Everdeen, no Scout Finch, no Princess Leia. But with Joan, there is also the danger of thrusting leadership onto girls not yet old enough to support themselves, or a parallel danger of projecting our own insecurities and fears onto the next generation, expecting them to solve things and clean up the messes we will leave behind. If Boomers pulled up the ladder behind them and Gen Xers leapt for the last rung, millennials and Gen Z women and girls are standing on the ground, trying to figure out what happened.

After the Parkland, Florida, school shootings and the March for Our Lives in 2018, when seventeen people were killed and a student-led group of hundreds of thousands of students marched on Washington, DC, to demand gun control, it wasn't uncommon to hear adults asking teenagers—who'd survived a mass trauma and been thrust into public roles before they could even drive a car or vote—to step up and fix things. At the UN, Thunberg laid into world leaders with a righteous anger. "You all come to us young people for hope," she told them. "How dare you? You have stolen my dreams and my childhood with your empty words, and yet I'm one of the lucky ones. People are suffering. People are dying."[2] Thunberg told the UN that young people would never forgive adults for the destruction they'd left behind.

And young women, too, often feel unforgiving of the situations they've been born into. At the college where I teach, we regularly have conversations about the fact that as long as we've known about the growing plague of sexual assault, we still put the onus on young women not to be assaulted, instead of teaching young men not to assault. We put the onus on young women for everything: to protect themselves, to lead us, to fix our messes, to help us understand ourselves. It is impossible these days for a woman to be old. It is equally impossible, in many ways, for a woman to be young.

———

I'm not a middle child but a penultimate child: the fourth of five. With each of my mother's pregnancies, my parents picked out a list of boy names, usually family names. It was the early sixties when they married, and they were both good Irish Catholic kids, hoping to compensate for the small families they'd each come from by producing a much larger one, preferably with enough men for the baseball and hockey teams my father obsessively followed. Baby one was a girl. A year later, baby two was a boy, but a year after that, baby three was a girl. Seven years later I materialized, baby number four, another girl. Seven years after that, my younger sister was born.

My father was an old-school, patriarchal-to-the-bone, pipe-smoking kind of guy, a heavy drinker and a heavy talker, and he needed nothing more than to frequently escape our creaky old house, with its single bathroom forcing us to shower in shifts and its wastebasket full of soiled menstrual supplies. He bought a VW Vanagon the year I was born and began stuffing all of us into it for long road trips, up the California coast, into and across Canada, and into the Alaskan wilderness.

When my older siblings outgrew the idea that it was in any way fun to be squeezed into a van that frequently broke down, spend weeks without showering, and use pit toilets while battling mosquitoes, it was just me and my younger sister and mom who went along. Then my mom had had enough and decided to keep my sister at home. So, from then on, it was just me and my father on the road for weeks and even months at a time, moving from campground to campground. I became semiferal for long stretches of time, and I'd go weeks without seeing another child. It was, in short, a very strange way to grow up.

I enjoy being alone. I even thrive on it—the stretches of time when I can write, read, think. After a long day of teaching at the university where I work, with enough students to populate a small city, if I can't come home and spend an hour or two by myself, I will mentally collapse. This is all probably a direct result of my childhood. Even within a large family, I was a small, isolated island, and as an adult, I look out at the world around me as if I were still stranded on that same island. It's not loneliness, most of the time, but it is a solitary nature antithetical to the way many people live.

In my years of girlhood, this independent, self-reliant streak was frequently commented upon as a kind of unusual maturity. An elementary school teacher told me I wrote "like a forty-year-old." In high school, a different teacher shrugged his shoulders one day and simply turned the class over to me, probably so he could go smoke a joint (I went to an "alternative" high school; this kind of thing happened a lot). When such maturity appeared in a girl, it was a quality people couldn't figure out how to handle.

As a teenager, I was more comfortable hanging out with college students, and in college, I fantasized about getting away from the self-involved, ego-trumpeting guys in lit classes and into graduate school—which turned out to be full of self-involved, ego-trumpeting guys too. Needless to say, they were always the professor's favorites.

Maturity for women is ill defined. Products targeted at "mature" women tend to fall into the AARP demographic—adult diapers and reading glasses and easy-to-open pill-sorting trays—and less to younger women who are, in fact, mature. In an era when men are rewarded for looking and acting younger than they really are, women who seem older than their years defy expectations in ways that confound advertisers.

Anyone who regularly spends time with young adults knows that mature girls are far from uncommon, so why are we shocked when girls rise up to lead, ask questions, and provoke response? Throughout history, girls had to be exceptional to be worthy of people's attention. For many centuries, patriarchal definitions of what made girls useful in society were usually whittled down to their potential future fecundity. Once girls began to be educated, exceptional girls went from being virgins and martyrs to being "mature" and "smart," but those labels were still attempts to conform girls to social expectations based on men's needs. A "mature" girl was ready to date and marry, and a "smart" girl was there to help her brother or husband or father. Just as older women are confined by the idea that they have outlived their usefulness to men, girls are still confined by the notion that their worth depends on that same usefulness.

The word *maturity* simply means that someone is "fully grown," but a girl who's passed through puberty isn't necessarily mature. We pressure girls to stay young and innocent even while bombarding them with media that pushes them into sexual exploration they may be ill prepared for. Or changing a climate in crisis—ditto. We ask them to grow up at the same time we tell them they are not grown up enough to make decisions of their own. We classify people as "young adults" until they are well into their forties, but at the same time, we warn young women that their biological clocks are ticking and they'd better get to reproducing before they waste those precious eggs; even if they don't want to reproduce, we encourage them to freeze those eggs just in case. We produce TV series about teen moms while scolding teenagers for being moms. We make it impossible, in other words, for women to grow up at the same time we discard them as soon as they are old.

———

In the second grade, every child at my Catholic elementary school, with its cracked, pink stucco walls and the rusty pipes in the bathroom foreshadowing the decay of the church it was attached to, was asked to write a book report about a saint. Our teacher gave us some books about saints with illustrations that made them all look like

Hummel figurines. Saint Francis, instead of being emaciated and clutching at his painful eyes, had cherubic pink cheeks and a goofy grin. Saint John the Baptist, who, we are told, ate locusts and wild honey, instead resembled a well-airbrushed Kenny Loggins. I, of course, turned to the page about Joan of Arc, saw a serious-faced girl in shiny armor sitting on a white horse, and fell in love. My middle name, which I only use for filing taxes, is Joan. But even more significantly, compared to Saint Therese of Lisieux, clutching a lily and cringing, or Saint Catherine of Siena, wagging a scolding finger, Joan of Arc looked like someone you wouldn't want to mess with. Yet, she was a girl like me—a child. It was romantic bait for an introverted religious kid, and I fell for it, turning in a book report that was three times the required length and heavy on florid adjectives and magic-markered fleur-de-lis in the margins. It was basically Catholic fan fiction. I probably got an A.

Knowing what I do now about hormones, puberty, and mental health, I can't help but think today that Joan was most likely bipolar, schizophrenic, or somewhere on the spectrum of mental illnesses. Some scholars posit she may have been epileptic; others point to the possibility that she drank unpasteurized milk, with parasites that caused damage to the frontal cortex. We just don't know. At fourteen, she began to have visions about a military victory. At sixteen, the Hundred Years' War was going badly enough that the king of France took a chance and appointed her the head of his army. At nineteen, after a trial that was politically motivated and botched, she was burned at the stake.

We know little about Joan's interior life other than what we can glean from the surviving court transcripts and contemporaneous accounts, but she was an illiterate child from the country, and one can't help but think that even if her religious fervor was real and ardent (she was, like most of her contemporaries, a zealous Catholic who was also a huge Islamophobe), some of those powerful men had manipulated her along the way. One of the things she was tried for was cross-dressing; Joan had insisted on wearing pants in prison because, had she worn a dress, she would have more easily been raped. During her trial, dressing in men's clothing was described as being "abominable to God." But the great men of the church would posthumously declare that this was forgivable, because she went back to wearing a dress afterward.

Women in Joan's time married as soon as they started menstruating and were primarily expected to cook, sew, till the fields, care for the livestock, have as many babies as possible, and die. So it's easy to understand why Joan became iconic as soon as the men who killed her realized they might have made a mistake: she was so outside of normative for her time that people were bound to want to understand what drove her.

Whether it's accurate or not, the men of the French jury that tried her are said to have watched her death, saying, "We have burned a saint." And speaking of accuracy,

Joan herself has been misquoted into oblivion. The "I am not afraid; I was born to do this" that's attributed to her and reproduced on mugs, bumper stickers, and jagged-lettered tattoos is wildly inaccurate. What she really said, during her trial, was "I do not fear men-at-arms; my way has been made plain before me."[3] What killed Joan, perhaps, was the fact that she dared to think for herself.

Joan's archetype in the Christian tradition is Mary, who, like Joan, has been blurred into a kind of pious, soft-focus version of the fiery, justice-minded Jewish girl she was more likely to have been, based on her Magnificat alone. That prayer in the Gospel of Luke, where Mary tells us about God's desire for a world where the rich are sent away empty-handed and the poor are raised up, where the humble are exulted and the prideful cast down, is a revolutionary vision for this young woman who grew up under the rule of an empire.

We know very little about who Mary really was, or even how old she was when she became pregnant, although the average age for marriage in her time was about thirteen or fourteen, so she was indeed likely young by modern standards. About the same age, in fact, as Joan of Arc when she began having visions.

While Mary's factual life may be a mystery, the all-male hierarchy of the Catholic church has turned her into an image of the perfect woman—pure, sinless, and self-abnegating—against whom, according to theologian Elizabeth Johnson, all other women are cast as sinful temptresses. In my childhood years of Catholic school, Mary's miraculous virginity was reiterated as a model for girls, something to somehow aspire to, even as the sexual revolution made it clear that very few people held onto their virginity until the end of high school, let alone until marriage. We were also taught that Mary retained her virginity until the end of her life, even though there are multiple references to Jesus's brothers and sisters. When we questioned this, the nuns told us they were probably her step-kids and quickly changed the subject.

In a head-spinning reversal, virginity in the popular culture of the seventies, eighties, and nineties was portrayed as a burden, a sign of squareness and immaturity. Girls lost their virginity in movies, on TV, and in those Judy Blume books we all read as a rite of passage. Teen sex was commonplace enough to mostly be no big deal, as long as they didn't get pregnant. But virginity in Christianity, especially Catholicism, was so aspirational, so often taught as something that would damn you to hell if you lost it, that this notion crowded out any meaningful form of sex education. To this day, in fundamentalist Christian communities, teen pregnancies are rampant. Even with three older siblings, I didn't know what the word *virginity* really meant until I transferred to a public school in fifth grade and a classmate told me that another of our classmates wasn't a virgin. When my face crumpled into an expression of confusion, she pointed me to the Judy Blume books in the library, with their penciled stars and creased corners on pages with sex scenes, and I finally understood.

This amalgamation of youth and sexual purity has had long-lasting and detrimental effects on women in just about every global culture and religion. To this day, virginity is still problematically viewed in dualistic ways that leave young girls in an untenable position. In *The Purity Myth*, Jessica Valenti writes that "women are pushing themselves and punishing themselves every day in order to fit into the narrow model of morality that virginity has afforded them."[4] Gender studies scholars have found that there are, on average, 2.9 million sexual insults hurled at women on Twitter every week.[5]

Girls in contemporary culture are simultaneously sexualized (in one stomach-churning example, twenty-five million incidents of child pornography, primarily featuring girls, are reported annually[6]) and shamed for their sexuality. This internal conflict about the value of our sexuality exists on the same spectrum with other self-esteem disorders, from body image issues to eating disorders to mental health issues. All of these have simmered and bubbled for thousands of years, thanks to patriarchal thinking and cultural expectations, and have spiked beyond anyone's expectations in recent years, fueled in no small part by social media.

The contemporary obsession with young women's sexuality, as steeped in puritanical American thinking as *The Scarlet Letter* and the Salem witch trials, is perhaps most familiar today to those in white evangelical mega-church circles. In the 1990s and early 2000s, purity rings, "True Love Waits" pledges, and an emphasis on modest dressing and avoiding any one-on-one contact with members of the opposite sex were widely taught as ways for girls (and, to a lesser extent, boys) to "save" themselves until marriage. The viral "Christian side hugs" video some people laughed at and thought was a parody was actually real and sincere. But the countereffect of purity culture was that girls who did indulge in sexual experimentation were often publicly shamed for it and sometimes, and particularly for queer Christian teens, kicked out of their churches and families.

Linda Kay Klein, who wrote a book about her own experiences of evangelical purity culture, told *Sojourners'* Sandi Villarreal, "I think there's a growing cognizance that [purity culture] didn't work." Klein says young evangelical women were shamed into being pure and then taught that staying pure would lead to a "fantastic, blissful life" with "awesome sex" in their marriages.[7] When this turned out not to be true and those marriages fell apart or settled into patterns of physical, sexual, or emotional abuse, those same women started showing signs of trauma: fight-or-flight responses, disassociation, and somatization (physical stress symptoms like racing heart rates, headaches, digestive issues, insomnia, and neck and back pain). Once the #MeToo movement began, the #ChurchToo movement wasn't far behind it, and close on the heels of #ChurchToo came #NoShame, helping victims of purity culture to reconstruct themselves in healthier relationships with their bodies.

For women like me in midlife or older, our bodies were at one point mostly seen as commodities. Whether or not we ever engaged in sex for pay, nearly every woman who's been with men has a story about being coerced or forced into sex or being made to feel guilty or shamed for not wanting it. Some of us have additional stories about being manipulated into sex in exchange for something: a job, a higher grade, keeping someone from dumping us. In patriarchal culture, men still hold much of the power in sexual relationships no matter how much sex-positive feminism has tried to give women back their sexual agency. And that's yet another reason so many young women have low self-esteem.

When one of my students wrote an essay on hookup culture among college students, she expected to hear that young women liked hooking up because of the sexual pleasure, that hookups gave them a sense of empowerment. What she found instead when she began interviewing people from her peer group were dozens of stories of college students—brilliant, creative, gifted young women, largely raised by feminist mothers—being talked into sex by guys (and sometimes being "roofied" or fed drinks until they passed out) who would go on to ghost them, leave them with STDs (which are on the rise, again, after tapering down during the AIDS epidemic), or leave them pregnant. And this was at a college where all students are lectured with regularity about consent, where birth control is freely available, and where Judith Butler, one of the most revered architects of gender theory in the world, is a member of the faculty. Sexual self-agency among young women is an important marker of how much feminism has changed things. But the crushing reality is that women's bodies are often still subject to abuse from men.

A youthful body is subject to the same critiques as any woman's body, and that critiquing can also be a form of policing and confinement. On social media, Rihanna's slim, toned body is tagged "aspirational" and "goals," and Adele's fuller figure is "relatable," at least until she appeared having lost a massive amount of weight, at which point she also became aspirational. The fat-positivity movement, the HAES (health at every size) movement, and other young performers like Lizzo have leaned into flipping the conversation to focus on self-esteem and on reclaiming our less-than-culturally-declared-norm-perfect bodies as something to be proud of. These people and movements are also up against advertising and media that funnel billions of dollars into the industry of making women of all ages feel bad about the way they look. And with young consumers as the most desired target for advertisers, they are winning the battle. Women don't just dislike their bodies; many of them hate themselves and think that's perfectly normal.

Even Mary and Joan of Arc's bodies did not belong to them. The obsessive reminders about Mary's virginity and the suspicious questioning of Joan's preference for wearing pants during her trial are just two among count-less examples of girls being turned into martyrs and saints, their bodies subject to gruesome forms of torture, from slicing off their breasts, to burning them at the stake, to plucking out their eyes and tying them up and throwing them into the sea, to feeding them to animals while they were still alive.

In every case, these young women's bodies were thought dangerous and had to be controlled. Even today, in the very strictest orders of Catholic nuns, young women entering the religious order are literally kept behind bars in the form of grilles that separate nuns from visitors, in addition to being under lock and key, not allowed to leave except for emergencies, in some cases for years. This is all theoretically voluntary, but the rule of life followed in most such communities that keeps them veiled, barefoot, and locked up was not written by women. It was written, thousands of years ago, by men.

———

What is it like to be a girl today? On the one hand, Elizabeth Warren would pinky swear with girls on the campaign trail that one day, they too might run for president. On the other hand, Elizabeth Warren was not the Democratic nominee in 2020. Girls and young women face the same pressures of patriarchal and misogynistic culture, reli-gion, and politics as in the past. But they also increasingly have strong female role models. More and more, they understand that the gender binary is largely a social construction. They have greater access now to opportunities that were far out of reach for previous generations.

From the early days of the entertainment industry until recently, female child stars were often tragic figures. Judy Garland, only twenty when she starred in *Meet Me in St. Louis,* was chewed up and spit out by Hollywood, a drug-addicted victim of the celebrity machine that created her. My generation grew up glued to *The Brady Bunch* but had no idea that Maureen McCormick, who played Marsha, struggled with severe depression. Drew Barrymore went to rehab at thirteen, and Lindsay Lohan and Britney Spears both struggled with drug addiction and untreated mental illness. In every case, these women were thrust into the spotlight too young to be in control of their image, their career, and their management.

The newer generation of child stars, activists, and young performers—like their peers Malala Yousafzai and Greta Thunberg—is, however, much more interested in self-control and self-agency. Billie Eilish, who released her first album at fifteen, self-produces much of her own music and directs her own videos. She also often wears baggy, gender-neutral clothing and dyes her own hair. Zendaya, who grew up in the Bay Area theater community, has also been able to have more control over her image and career, firing back at racist critics and standing up for herself on social media. And the girls from the cast of *Stranger Things*, one of the most virally popular shows in recent years, are mature and self-expressive in ways that surprise people who don't regularly interact with girls and young women. Millennials and Gen Z kids alike, with a more diverse cast of role models and greater opportunities for self-invention, may face the same social dilemmas as older generations, but they have a greater arsenal of tools at their disposal.

The 2018 election upset of Alexandria Ocasio-Cortez, the youngest-ever member of Congress, is another example of how younger women are using their positioning between the patriarchal structures of the past and what will hopefully be a more equitable future as a springboard for change. Ocasio-Cortez combined campaign strategies from the past—going door-to-door to get to know her constituents and ask for votes—with savvy, millennial-style use of Twitter to clap back at critics. Greta Thunberg's platform began with an old-fashioned school strike where she simply walked out and held a sign, but it quickly expanded to the internet as well. For all of the damage social media is capable of doing to girls, they understand how to harness its power. The March for Our Lives started as a hashtag and expanded into a national movement. So did #MeToo. So did Black Lives Matter, which was also started by three Black women.

Young women today are held back by the same antiquated binary ideas about gender as the generations before them, even as those binaries are falling away. For many centuries, conviction was thought to have a gender, and it was male. But the recognition of Malala Yousafzai and Greta Thunberg as leaders not despite their age and gender but because of them may indicate we are finally ready to listen to girls. In that sense, perhaps Joan of Arc can be reclaimed as well—not as a religious martyr with some questionable beliefs, but as an example of a young woman who followed her instincts and defied stereotypes. As an example of what courage can be.

———

A few years ago, I was in downtown Los Angeles for a book reading, with some time to kill beforehand. It was blazingly hot, and I walked over to the Cathedral of Our Lady of Angels—on the outside, a chunky modernist building, but on the inside, an airy, clean space, with enough cool air for an overheated Northern Californian like me. All along the walls of the cathedral are massive tapestries depicting saints facing the altar. But the artist, an Angeleno named John Nava, doesn't portray the saints as brittle figures from antiquity. Instead, he went around Los Angeles taking pictures of people with a camera. So the cathedral's tapestry saints are really just normal people from LA, all different races and all different ages, in contemporary dress and robes that could be from any era.

Among them, I was drawn to a serious-faced young woman with cropped hair, her head leaning into her folded hands, and sure enough, on the pamphlet I'd taken from an entryway table, she was identified as Joan of Arc. Just another girl, another person evolving into maturity, into a sense of understanding herself, caught in a moment of contemplation, worry, or prayer; caught in between youth and adulthood, between other people's expectations and the moment of her own self-discovery.

TWO

OLD

A few months after I turned forty-eight, I woke up at three a.m. on a weekday and choked down a bottle of white-grape–flavored carbohydrate fasting beverage, its label puzzlingly recommending its use for both surgeries and marathon running. The night before, as per instructions, I'd showered, wiped down my entire body with antibacterial cloths, and swallowed two gabapentin pills. My skin was still sticky as I stumbled around the dark house in the morning, trying to drink as much water as possible. It was unclear when I'd be able to eat or drink again. At four a.m., I arrived at a hospital in an industrial area beyond the suburbs, where I sat in a waiting room with a half-dozen other people waiting to have surgery.

For more than a year leading up to this, I'd been having painful and, frankly, disgusting medical symptoms. My periods, always excruciatingly heavy, had begun to last for ten, fifteen, or twenty days. My sleep was disrupted as I had to get up multiple times every night to swallow more Advil or mop up the blood that soaked through the sheets and into the mattress. Sometimes I'd bleed so much I got dizzy at work or had to sleep lying on a towel. A year and six pelvic scans later, it was clear that one of my ovaries had a cyst the size of a chicken egg and the other had two more cysts, each nearly as big. After one ruptured on a rainy night that March, ER scans revealed that the lining of my uterus was abnormally plush with errant cells, hiding six fibroids.

My surgeon, a tough-talking New Yorker, took one look at my scans and said it all had to go. The left ovary, the fallopian tubes, the uterus, and the cervix. We bargained for my remaining ovary like it was the subject of an eBay bidding war.

The surgery took five hours. It was supposed to take two, but my innards were so riddled with endometriosis— an estrogen-fueled condition where the uterus sheds cells all over the pelvic cavity—that the surgeon had to excise deposits from my bowels and bladder. The ruptured ovarian cyst had splattered toxic deposits everywhere. It was, by all accounts, gruesome. I did not have cancer, thankfully. Yet, like many women, I'd pushed through decades of pain and catastrophic bleeding every month, thinking this was just what happened with age.

When I woke up in the recovery room groggy and confused, a nurse patted my arm and reminded me I'd just had a hysterectomy. The woman next to me began vomiting loudly, over and over again, and I sank back into a fog.

Suddenly, I was old.

Technically, this is not true. Forty-eight is not old in America today. A hundred years ago, it might have been, but hopefully, I can expect to live a bit longer. However, for women, the end date on our reproductive cycles has traditionally been seen as the beginning of our decline. And just as I sat down to start writing this book, COVID-19 began scything its way around the world. While it sometimes found younger victims, the greatest danger it posed was to the old. Doctors had to choose whether to keep ventilating a person who might live another decade or a person who might live several more. One of my students, a former paramedic in his fifties, once told me that realistically, if there were a mass shooting at the university where I teach, paramedics would save the youngest students first, not anyone over thirty. We would both be goners, he said.

The old are disposable. Women are used to hearing stories of the social invisibility of middle age and being elderly, the steady erasure of our sexual selves becoming a larger erasure of our very identities. How we react to this varies wildly. Some women become louder, more deliberately obnoxious, Klaxons firing off warnings to the young about what's headed their way. Others use their invisibility as a kind of superpower, one where their disappearance becomes the means by which they get more done, change more lives, and become the people they'd patiently been waiting to be.

But our collective ageism and habitual moving of the older, the louder, the disappearing into even more marginalizing homes or planned communities where they can't be seen or heard by the rest of us is something I became acutely aware of as my body began to change after surgery. My remaining ovary started to wind down, bringing on night sweats and hot flashes right as a pandemic whose main symptom is fever swept over the world. My eyes got worse, my hair got grayer, and I was perpetually cranky and tired.

There was no great wisdom in any of this. Before I had surgery, I'd written down a list of things I wanted to do when I recovered, and somewhere on the list was mentoring young women. But my students increasingly treated me like a regular grown-up rather than the cool, tattooed older-sister character I'd been able to play for decades. As we Gen Xers slid into our fifties, my students' parents had plenty of tattoos of their own and a catalog knowledge of golden-age nineties hip-hop that outshone mine. It seemed I was just another third-wave feminist gliding toward the crone years.

The problem is that I live in the land of the purple people. In the Bay Area, women over fifty or so tend to move into what I think of as the "Eileen Fisher years" if they're upper-middle class or wealthy. This is the kind of woman who's typically employed as a therapist, environmental lawyer, tenured professor, or academic administrator. She stopped dyeing her hair years ago and wears chunky eyeglass frames she got while on vacation in Amsterdam, along with cropped wide-leg pants with an elastic waist and a flowing neutral-colored tunic. She has an annual subscription to a local theater company and her partner is someone similarly employed, so their income is formidable. Of course, she drives a Prius but secretly wants to trade up for a Tesla. She sends her kids to small liberal-arts colleges, reads the *New Yorker*, and is still pissed about what happened to Hillary, but in a polite, complaining-after-two-glasses-of-wine kind of way.

If they're middle class or lower-middle class, women in the Bay Area often turn into "purple people." Purple people are the former Deadheads, the ones who want to fight you over the last zucchini at Berkeley Bowl, the ones driving a Volvo station wagon with 200K miles on it that's somehow still running. Purple people are the ones canvassing in front of the grocery store and nurturing their three legal pot plants in the backyard. They have a framed copy of the poem "When I Am an Old Woman I Shall Wear Purple" somewhere in their home and show up at city council meetings to yell about stop signs. As much as I know and love many Eileen Fisher moms and purple people, I don't want to become any of them.

The fact is that women in my generation, and most women in general, are in fact lacking in practical role models for what it means to be middle aged or old, to grow into eras of life we don't have a context for. Jung's archetype of the wise old woman is not a benevolent grandma living in a cottage in the woods but something closer to the Hindu goddess Kali: destroyer and creator, generative and capable of erasing the world. Get on Kali's bad side, and she'll add your skull to the string around her neck. Get on her good side, and she'll protect you with a lioness's ferocity. Kali also represents the kind of aggressive feminism that was more common to Gen Xers, who preferred being downwardly mobile DIY zine-producing Riot Grrrls to striving Ms. magazine readers.

But Kali does not grow old. She remains young, blue, and angry forever.

When I say that my hysterectomy made me old, I mean that it was a terminal point in my life. I tried and failed, multiple times, to find anyone close to my age who'd had the same surgery, finding only peppy websites like Hys-terSisters, with you-go-girl chatter about "how hubby can help" and what kind of compression panties you'd want to wear when you felt like your guts were about to fall out. A third of women in America have hysterectomies, but none of them seem to want to talk about it with any sense of honesty. Spending two weeks shuffling around the house with an ice pack shoved down into the front of my sweatpants, I did not want a cheerleader. I did not want to be reassured I was still feminine and desirable. After a year of having six pelvic ultrasounds, with total strangers shoving a lubed wand into parts of my body I'd generally rather not have a conversation about, what I wanted was for nobody to touch me ever again.

My mother and grandmother had both had the same surgery at the same age as I did. This coincidence some-times comes back to me as evidence that God has a weird sense of humor. Yet when I tried to remember what it was like for my mom, I could only vaguely recall the take-out food my father fed us for several weeks when she was too sore and tired to cook. And the surgery itself has evolved radically in the past few decades. My mother and grand-mother had invasive abdominal procedures, versus my laparoscopic one, and were both put on hormone replace-ment at doses we now know put women at a higher risk for heart attacks, stroke, and breast cancer.

I was sent home with a sheaf of paperwork about pain killers, hormone blockers, hormone replacement, when to start driving a car again, but almost nothing about what this reconfigured body might mean for my mind. In the car on the way home, fighting back the urge to vomit, I knew life was going to be different. But *how* would remain unclear for some time.

Our understandings of how the uterus works are clearer today than they were in the past. But they're still grounded in centuries of men speculating and guessing about women's bodies, often to devastating effect. The Greek word for uterus, after all, was *hysterika*. Plato and Hippocrates believed that women were a mutant version of men, and that our uteruses were able to physically drift around inside our bodies, which caused us to behave erratically, a problem that worsened as we aged (women in ancient Greece only lived about thirty-five years on average, so who knows whether most of them even made it to menopause?). The Greek physician Aretaeus of Cappadocia wrote that the uterus "delights also in fragrant smells, and advances towards them; and it has an aversion to foetid smells, and flees from them, and on the whole it is like an animal within an animal."[1] Greek physicians treated women's physical ailments by waving lavender around their abdomens to entice the errant uterus to return to its rightful place.

The Romans weren't much better about understanding the uterus. The Greek physician Galen thought that built-up menstrual blood would suffocate the uterus and cause it to send off a noxious cloud that would gradually poison the other organs (which, to give him some credit, does sound a little like endometriosis). By the Victorian era, doctors treated women for mental health issues by shooting jets of water at their abdomens or using vibrators to provoke orgasms that were thought to cure hysteria.

Age is madness. And it's true that our uteruses can drive us mad. When the photographer Elinor Carucci had a hysterectomy in her forties, she told *Wired* magazine in 2019 that it spurred a reckoning about age. "It was like, 'I woke up this morning with a uterus, and now, a few hours later, I don't have one and never will.'" Carucci asked her surgeon if she could photograph the uterus before it was sent to medical waste, and the photo is jarring—and beautiful. The uterus is splayed on a blue medical towel, a bright pink orb with the severed fallopian tubes neatly arranged on either side. It looks like the body of a squid: rounded on top with tentacles of flesh hanging down, the ribbons of the cervix, which is shredded during the surgery so it can be removed. Carucci said she felt compelled to look at her uterus, to see it for the first time, "and part of it was damaging," she added. "It was just really hard for me to see."[2]

At my postsurgical appointment, my surgeon clapped her hands together with the enthusiasm of someone who's removed a million uteruses as she suggested showing me the photos of the surgery so I could get a closer look at how damaged I'd really been. I declined.

A couple weeks later, I was sent the pathology report. This was easier to cope with; it was just words. In clinical language, the pathologist laid out what she'd found. All of my malfunctioning reproductive system was sent to be incinerated. I'd never felt a particular drive to have kids but understood now that it probably never would have happened anyway; my DNA had handed me the equivalent of a reproductive trash heap, and now it had all gone up in smoke.

———

Our understanding of aging is right in the middle of a Venn diagram's intersection of spirituality, culture, and medicine. Our spiritual lives—the grounding by which many of us understand the world as older women—are solely lacking in role models. Western religions are skimpy on depictions of women, period. And skimpier in their depictions of older women. And even fewer of the few are positive, awe-inspiring, kick-ass depictions. In the Scriptures, there are a few older women like Sarah and Elizabeth, but in contrast to younger women like Esther and Tamar, they mostly play backing roles as the wives of prophets.

We know Mary is probably quite young when Jesus is born, and there are scant examples of older women in the New Testament. Among these, one of the most intriguing characters is Anna, a prophetess who shows up after the birth of Jesus at the same time as Simeon, the Jewish elder who gets to recite an entire canticle, what will come to be known as the *Nunc Dimittis*.

Anna, on the other hand, doesn't even get to speak in her own voice. Her words are paraphrased in the text, rather than quoted. As an elder, she actually outranks Simeon because he's captured in the act of making a prophecy, whereas she's already known around the temple as a prophetess. In a single short paragraph, we learn that she's from the tribe of Asher, that she "never left the temple but worshiped night and day" (Luke 2:37).

This pious model of an old woman giving her entire life over to prayer is sweet and, perhaps for some people, even inspirational. But it's yet another example of the patriarchal tendency to strip women of their own voices, and to have their narratives erased down to skeletal outlines that inspired the male authors of the books. Luke's Gospel says Anna was eighty-four years old at the time of Jesus's presentation and had been living in the temple for quite some time. Elders were venerated in Mediterranean culture mostly because people just did not live very long in Jesus's era. The average woman made it to thirty if she was lucky enough not to die in childbirth, and the Bible isn't really great about accuracy when it comes to people's life spans. Methuselah's 969 years were likely something more like fifty.

In the Quran, a woman who has passed through menopause is a Qawa'id, which Imam Ibn Kathir tells us translates to "those women who . . . no longer have any desire for marriage" or "those women from whom desire and sexual passion is not (typically) required."[3] It's easy to imagine that this is a kind of liberation. Freed from expectations about sex and sexuality, any woman can embrace a more prophetic, more independent identity. But who was actually listening to these female elders? Anna exits the stage after her cameo appearance and is never seen again. And while I'm not an expert on Islam, it's not hard to imagine that those Muslim women who've passed through their fertile years might also be relegated to a background role, just as postfertile women are in almost every culture.

On the other hand, while Western religions have thin offerings to provide models for women as we age, Native Americans have, for thousands of years, been guided by wisdom figures like Grandmother Spider. In the Hopi creation story, it is the elderly Spider Woman who imbues humans with souls. She became such a powerful figure that her mythology spread like her cast webs among Native tribes, from the Southwest up into the Northwest, the Midwest, and up and down the East Coast. But many Native tribes are also matriarchal, which is not the case in Western religions.

Patriarchy has long tried to root out any female gods who would help us understand how to navigate transitional times of life. The suppression of Gnostic images of God as Sophia, God's partner in creation, for example, was just the beginning of centuries of Western erasure of women from creation stories. The Gnostics were among the many groups of early Christians later dismissed as kooks. But the Gnostics thought that a male God couldn't possibly be capable of procreation on his own, so they gave him a partner. In the Nag Hammadi texts, discovered in Egypt in the 1940s, the Gnostic Sophia is presented both as God's female partner in creation and as Jesus's female spiritual twin as well as the Holy Spirit (it's easy to make a joke here about women and multitasking). The Roman Catholic Church, however, swiftly dismissed those texts as heresies, and aside from Dan Brown awkwardly trying to resurrect these ideas in *The Da Vinci Code*, most modern Christians know little to nothing about this hidden part of their history.

Without women present (or allowed to speak and record) at the moment of creation, how are we supposed to know how to grow old? Imagine if the ceiling of the Sistine Chapel had a depiction of an old woman touching Adam's finger, as the Afro-Cuban-American artist Harmonia Rosales has painted. In Rosales's depiction, that old woman is brown, and the finger she's touching is a woman's finger. That finger belongs to a woman who is also brown. But we got an old white God with a long white beard instead, almost touching the finger of a white man, and much has gone wrong with Christianity ever since.

Literature has often followed suit. Our literary and cultural models for aging women suffer from the same problems of silencing and erasure. But they also play into the same stereotypes of hags, crones, overly ambitious manipulators, and horny old broads. Shakespeare, who conjured up dozens of brilliant, bold, and courageous older male characters, and whose work remains an inescapable influence on almost all of Western literature, barely has a couple of handfuls of female characters in the entire canon of plays he wrote, and very few of them are old. Because women's roles were played by adolescent boys on Shakespeare's stages, perhaps this is just a casting problem. But even a contemporary actor as eminent as Helen Mirren says she doesn't play Shakespeare roles anymore simply because there aren't enough of them for a woman of her age.

Ashley "Aley" O'Mara of Syracuse University says that part of the way Shakespeare writes older women stems from the Renaissance view that "old" simply meant anyone who was either postmenopausal or incapable of (or uninterested in) bearing a child. But women in that era went through menopause earlier, so the toothless, elderly nurse in *Romeo and Juliet* might be forty, tops. O'Mara adds that this meant older women were seen as more masculine and more androgynous, because they were no longer capable of being mothers and motherhood was associated with care and compassion. When their reproductive systems stopped working, they essentially became more like men. They stopped being nurturing and started being ambitious. But those same ambitious women in Shakespeare became villainous caricatures like Lady Macbeth, regularly invoked today as a trope of what goes wrong when an older woman stops caring about what people think.

When we think about the idea of "strong" female characters in literature, the lists inevitably skew to the young. Hermione Granger of the Harry Potter series, Katniss Everdeen from *The Hunger Games*, Eowyn in *Lord of the Rings*, Arya Stark in the Game of Thrones books, Jo March in *Little Women*, *Pride and Prejudice*'s Elizabeth Bennet, Nancy Drew, Celie in *The Color Purple*, Hester Prynne in *The Scarlet Letter*, and Janie Crawford in *Their Eyes Were Watching God* are all young. Teenagers, in many cases. Some of those books were written by men, but many were written by women. Jane Austen, beloved as she may be, reduces Mrs. Bennet and most of the older women in her novels to nattering neurotic clichés, and the mothers of many of these other powerful young women are dead, often forcing the characters to discover their own agency under the tutelage of men rather than women. So we end up with a literary canon of strong female characters who are seen as strong primarily because they hang out with dudes.

Where are the older women who might have also mentored them? Obviously, those characters weren't as interesting or worthy of development. Or maybe it was an issue of trying to attract readers. In the Harry Potter books, teenage Hermione can simultaneously be smart, courageous, and pretty, but the older female teachers McGonagall, Trelawney, and Sprout are, respectively, bitchy, kooky, and barely fleshed out into three dimensions. Those books were written for kids, to be sure, but every kid has a grandparent, or a teacher, or a family doctor of a certain age.

The problem with being a woman who ages today is that while we grew up without good role models for getting older, we are also expected to be able to do everything at once. The second wave of feminism was so focused on breaking women out of housekeeping and into the workplace that it ended up putting our mothers into the same impossible position many of us are in, of constantly having to choose between career and family, between a creative life and financial well-being, between selfishness and selflessness. These binary positions are both false and untenable.

In the pandemic days of lockdown that unfolded as I wrote this chapter, many friends with children were home-schooling for the first time, involuntarily, while they simultaneously tried to work, take care of their own aging parents, and handle the barrage of horrific news. None of us was sleeping; all of us were barely holding on. And even before COVID-19, the expectation has increasingly been that if women want to "have it all," they have to put up with it all.

What happened to Hillary Clinton epitomizes this problem with our incapacity to know what to make of older women, and it happened again in 2020 with Elizabeth Warren. In both cases, women who were the best qualified, the most capable, and the best primed to fix the problems left behind by previous presidential administrations led by men were shunned at the voting booth. Yes, Hillary won the popular vote, and for a brief moment Warren led the overcrowded race of Democrats. But their accomplishments, which took decades to achieve, actually worked against them.

Women who are high achievers have to gain a certain sense of competence, and that pushes back against the crone/kook/bosomy grandmother trifecta into which older women are slotted. In the same historical era when Angela Merkel led Germany, Nancy Pelosi led the house, Ruth Bader Ginsburg sat on the Supreme Court, and Queen Elizabeth II was the longest-reigning ruler in the British monarchy, America cringed at the idea of a competent older woman being president.

This is complicated yet again by the messaging that we need to "own" our age, at the same time that we're told we have to fight it. Once you feed Facebook or Instagram your birth date, you're hit with advertising that pushes this both ways. On the one hand, I get told I need to embrace aging by buying hip-looking reading glasses, because women are in need of an "eyewear rebellion." On the other hand, perhaps I'm interested in having the fat underneath my chin surgically sucked out, or I'd like to pay thousands of dollars for a series of painful injections that will smooth away the creased evidence around my mouth and eyes that I have to juggle two full-time jobs in order to pay rent. I'm told that "grombre" is the new thing, and that women are growing out their gray roots to an ombre effect and sporting them proudly, but I'm also told home hair-color kits can reverse this trend while still keeping me looking "natural."

A few years ago, I was on a flight to Chicago when a wiggly line materialized in my vision. Alarmed it might be a stroke, I paid $8 for in-flight wi-fi to Google it, only to discover it was most likely a floater, a clump of cells that forms in the viscous fluid of the eyeball. A few weeks later, I saw an ophthalmologist who confirmed this and reminded me that "once you start adding up those birthdays," all kinds of weird, unexpected things would start happening. And they did.

In movies and on TV, this is treated as the Janus face of comedy and tragedy. The woman character who's getting older is either dying of breast cancer or racing to the freezer to stick her head in when a hot flash hits. In my experience, physical decline is more like a car you keep driving because you can't afford to replace it. Back pain isn't funny and mammograms aren't always tragic, but when the anesthesiologist told me I was "young and healthy" at forty-eight, I had to laugh, even though I was doped up out of my mind. My "young and healthy" reproductive system was about to be put in a bag, sliced into ribbons, and then sucked out through tubes. It was almost actually funny. It was almost actually sad.

There are some signs of change. TV and films are adapting at a decent clip to the reality that older women are interesting. *The Crown, Killing Eve, Happy Valley, Watchmen, One Day at a Time*, a slew of BBC crime shows, and many more recent series have female leads in their forties and fifties. The 2019 movie *The Favourite* had two female leads in their late forties, and Laura Dern, in her early fifties, was the only performer among the ensemble of mostly younger actresses in *Little Women* to win an Oscar. Granted, these TV and film leads are much smoother-skinned and a lot thinner than many of us in their age demographic. But watching fifty-year-old Regina King beating the crap out of racists on *Watchmen* has a level of satisfaction that's missing from watching a man in the same age group do the same thing. Maybe, just maybe, we've finally come into our own to the point that we're allowed to kick other people's asses.

And if we look backward, we can also find examples of women who stepped into the fullness of vocation and vision in their older years. They're just not always easy to find. Near my house in Oakland is a modest storefront that houses the Ella Baker Center for Human Rights, a nonprofit advocacy group. Baker, who was born in 1903 as the granddaughter of a slave, spent years working with the NAACP on economic justice campaigns. But it was in her fifties and sixties, as the civil rights movement grew, that she took up leadership positions in the Student Nonviolent Coordinating Committee and participated in direct nonviolent actions throughout the Freedom Rides and Freedom Summer. Older than most of the ministers she worked with, including Rev. Dr. Martin Luther King Jr., Baker was vocally critical of sexism in the civil rights movement, mentoring and supporting many

younger women, including Angela Davis. Baker continued her activism into her eighties, yet like many women
in the movement, she was relegated to a background role
even while holding leadership positions. Even so, Baker's
drive to change the world shone through anyway. "Give
people light," she said in 1944, "and they will find the way."

At the turn of the twentieth century, the community
and union organizer Mother Jones was called "the most
dangerous woman in America" because of her ability to
rally and organize workers. At that point, she was in her
sixties. The Catholic Worker Movement founder Dorothy Day was still being arrested at protests until shortly
before she died at the age of eighty-three. George Eliot,
Annie Proulx, and Toni Morrison are among the women
who didn't publish their first novels until they were over
forty. Donna Shalala was elected to Congress at the age
of seventy-seven in 2019. Boomers, Gen Xers, millennials, and zoomers alike today love Dolly Parton and reruns
of *The Golden Girls*. But every exceptional example of
an older woman still runs up against the same fears and
misconceptions of aging that have held women back for
generations.

Perhaps growing older is just another example of the
liminal space occupied by millions of women around
the world. Once you step out of the socially constructed
boundaries around ideas of what makes a woman a
woman no matter what her age, you enter a space where
you're pretty much left to figure things out on your own.

For most of your life, you are told you're too young, and then one day, you wake up and the world has decided you're not young anymore.

As we get older, that has its advantages. We are more competent, and confident. But it's also painful and isolating and strange to feel your body and mind changing and to watch people reacting to that. Younger women today may be learning more about what happens as you get older thanks to a few taboos about aging falling away, but they're pressured just as much as any previous generation to stay young. Age is a gift, but it's also a burden, and in between those two things are just the days we move through as we try to determine the direction we're headed.

A year after my hysterectomy, the small scars on my abdomen have pretty much faded away. It took six months before I cleaned out my "period drawer," with its supplies of tampons and pads, and donated the unopened boxes to a women's shelter. There was a strange grief to that too, coupled with a sense of liberation. I was free from the pain and bleeding that had marked my life on a regular basis for decades, but I was also, clearly, no longer young. One part of my life had been traded for another, newer, stranger one. I had arrived, like so many other women, in the land of the liminal.

THREE

CRAZY

I n 1943, the philosopher and mystic Simone Weil died at the age of thirty-four. As with many dead women, there is both consensus and disagreement about what led to her death, but the method of it is clear: she deliberately starved herself. Weil, who was raised in an agnostic Jewish family, had a powerful religious experience in 1937. In the tiny chapel known as the Portiuncula in Assisi, Italy, the same chapel where Saint Francis heard God's voice telling him to rebuild the church, she experienced what some scholars call a "religious ecstasy"—the kind of transcendent, out-of-body experience people have tried to put words to for centuries.

For the few years that remained of her life, Weil tried to balance her powerful religious impulse with her work as a covert operative during World War II and her writings in philosophy. It's been rumored but never confirmed that Weil was baptized as a Catholic. Her religious interests were too wide-ranging for her to be entirely comfortable being pinned to one tradition, so she remained religiously defiant and in-between. She was Catholic-attracted at any rate, and part of that attraction was deeply embedded in her desire to understand the suffering of Jesus, in large part because she lived in an era when suffering was all around her. This moved Weil to try to physically embody the world's suffering, to experience its deprivation and pain. Like many women mystics, Weil understood the relationship with God as a quid pro quo. In *Gravity and Grace*, she wrote that "love of God is pure when joy and suffering inspire an equal degree of gratitude."[1]

But why did she deliberately starve herself? Part of it was a desire to align her own suffering with the poorest of the poor during the war. A part also bears similarity to what medieval people knew as *anorexia mirabilis*, holy anorexia, where they attributed a miraculous loss of appetite to a person's religious fervor. Many male medieval saints undertook physical punishments (often self-inflicted) and vows of chastity in order to grow closer to the sufferings of Christ, while some female medieval saints went to extremes in fasting instead. At the time, the church fathers attributed this loss of appetite to God's grace, but many of these women died painfully and young as the result of this "miraculous" lack of appetite. Today, holy anorexia, like other eating disorders, would very likely be classified as a form of mental illness.

In fact, the life stories of any number of women mystics can sound to the modern ear like a catalog of entries in the DSM-5, the manual mental health professionals use to diagnose patients. Weil and other mystics saw their lives as a battle between good and evil, with their minds and bodies enduring sufferings they translated as self-sacrificial offerings to God. Describing something of her experience that sounds to the twenty-first-century ear like severe depression, Weil tells us that that which is "gloomy, monotonous, barren, boring" is evil.[2]

Weil's equal attractions to God, social justice, and philosophy have made her, whom many regard as a genius, an increasingly fascinating subject for feminist scholars in the years since her death. Like many women, her work was not much known during her lifetime, which also relates in part to a larger problem: Why are so many gifted women battered by their own minds, trapped in a liminal space between the demons of their own imaginations and the hope for their mental suffering to reach an end through treatment, medication, or even death?

Fifty years after Weil died, something much less interesting happened. I earned a bachelor's degree in English. Four years later, I added an MFA in creative writing. Back then, my writing was focused on poetry, and with the encouragement of professors who saw me as a potential big fish in the minuscule pond of my Catholic liberal arts college, I'd planned on riding the academic wave all the way through a PhD. This did not happen. Within three years of graduating, I was permanently soured on writing poetry, had declined admission to the doctoral programs where I'd been accepted, and was even miserable browsing bookstores, something that—much to my embarrassment as a writer who's supposed to love them—I'm still unable to do with any kind of pleasure.

The story of the person who drops out of academia is commonplace. The job market is dire, the prospects for humanities PhDs negligible, and "I quit academia" essays and books have become a genre unto itself: quit lit. However, I am, technically, an academic. Without a doctorate, I worked and published my way into a job teaching writing full-time at a well-regarded public university, and today, I regularly attend conferences where I present papers and give invited talks, occasionally advise grad students on their theses, and review essays for academic journals.

But I'm not "Doctor Oakes." That's my oldest sister, who's an MD. To my students and people at conferences who call me "Doctor," I reply, "Call me Kaya," because that's who I am: Kaya, an under-credentialed writer who lucked into a career. Like many other women, I experience impostor syndrome daily, and thus, I don't *really* qualify as an academic. I don't *really* belong at my job, and I certainly don't deserve it, because I failed the Credentialism Olympics.

The roots of that failure can be traced to those undergrad intro-to-lit courses every English major takes. Like so many other students who fell into this trap of believing we were meant for greater things, I loved the whispery thin pages of the Norton Anthologies; loved how I could read three, four, five times the assigned length from classes and never tire of it; loved how easily I earned As and how my professors, for the most part, treated me like an intellectual peer rather than the irritating, pretentious undergrad I really was.

But those Norton Anthologies were full of secrets, ones that it would take a long time to fully understand. There were, of course, not many women writers included in them, and even if many of my professors were women, they struggled to assemble syllabi that reflected back the demographic makeup of their classes. In the 1990s, more than half the students at my college were female, but we were also in the thick of the canon wars, with half the faculty sticking up for the dead-white-guy syllabus and the other half battling to include more women and writers of color. But the women writers in the Norton Anthologies had one thing in common, aside from their gender. They were all crazy.

As it turns out, so am I.

The patron saint of mental health in the Catholic church is Saint Dymphna. Did we learn about her in my years of Catholic school? Probably not. I text two Catholic women friends who are also writers and ask, "Can you think of women saints who were mentally ill?" Within seconds, my phone screen fills up, a litany of the crazed. Saint Agnes. Saint Angela of Foligno. Bernadette. Margaret of Cortona. My old hero Joan of Arc. My friend Jessica mentions Saint Dymphna, but says she never really learned why she was assigned as patron to the mentally ill. So I start digging in, and I learn this:

Once upon a time in the seventh century, when Ireland was partially populated by Catholics who had been converted by missionaries and partially by Celtic pagan polytheists still clinging to their native religion, a pagan king of a region called Oriel fell in love with a devout Christian woman and married her. Their daughter Dymphna took a vow of chastity at fourteen, and shortly after, her mother died. Her father was urged to remarry, but because Dymphna looked so much like her late mother, the king began to exhibit signs of madness and decided to sexually pursue his own daughter. Dymphna fled to what's now Belgium, where she used her family money to establish a home for the poor and sick. Her use of Celtic coins helped her father trace her to her new home, so he traveled there and cut off her head. She was fifteen years old. The end.

Why did the church fathers decide that a victim of incest would make a good patron for people struggling with anxiety, depression, and everything else on the spectrum of mental health? Because, of course, the church is so terrified of women's sexuality that it would rather appoint someone who successfully guarded her virginity but was a victim of another's mental illness as the patron of the mentally ill than a person who actually struggled with mental illness.

Dymphna is often depicted holding the same white lilies that all chaste saints hold as a visual symbol. But even if her father was mentally ill and even if mental illness is at least partly hereditary, there's no evidence that Dymphna was mentally ill herself. So why her, and why not any of the mystics and visionaries and women holding their plucked-out eyes on a plate like Saint Lucy or their severed breasts on a plate like Saint Agnes, or Christina the Astonishing flying into the church rafters, or any of those holy mad fools for God? Because the church loves women who are victims. And the same is true in college English courses, but instead of plucked-out eyes and flying saints, we got syllabi full of women writers who were anxious and depressed.

By the time I finished my MFA, I told my advisor, a brilliant poet whom I looked up to like you do when you're young and meet someone whose life you wouldn't mind stepping into, that if anyone ever brought up Sylvia Plath in a classroom again, I would probably explode. It was the nineties, we had played in the fields of feminism for decades, Riot Grrrls were stomping around in boots and bras with no shirts worn over them, and yet, my classmates still invoked Plath with a regularity that made me queasy. The problem wasn't Plath herself or her writing. It was the way we were taught to talk about her, which always centered on her depression and the fact that she died by suicide. We weren't talking about her husband Ted Hughes's infidelities, or the letters to her psychologist that would turn up years later revealing Hughes had beaten Plath while she was pregnant, causing a miscarriage, and told her he wished she were dead. We were instead talking about how she gassed herself with her children in the room next door, leaving them milk and bread to eat. We knew those details, acutely. We talked about Plath as a victim of her own mind. Our conversations about her in classes were exhausting, demoralizing, and dangerously contagious.

We said the same things about Virginia Woolf and the rocks in her pockets, Anne Sexton, Charlotte Perkins Gilman, and the Beat writer Elise Cowan, who is best known for typing out her ex-boyfriend Allen Ginsberg's poem "Kaddish" before Ginsberg came to terms with being gay and rejected her. She jumped out of a seventh-floor window.

Then we talked about women writers who *might* have been crazy. How did Mary Shelley manage to think up Frankenstein? How did Emily Dickinson cope with her self-imposed isolation? Why did Marina Tsvetaeva return to Russia from a life in Paris when she knew the Russian government would make her life so unbearable she'd end it by hanging herself? We talked about this so impartially, with a mind to finding evidence in "the work," prying apart poetry and fiction and essays to look for clues, tracing a trail of breadcrumbs that led from troubled childhoods to the inevitable breakdowns, stints in mental hospitals, night terrors, broken relationships, abandoned children, death. It was our job to explain that this is what it meant to be a woman writer: you had to be crazy. All of them were.

In 2001, the psychologist James C. Kaufman described this phenomenon as "the Plath effect" (there she is again). Female poets, according to Kaufman, are more likely to experience mental illness than women who write in any other genre. Women writers, generally, are more likely than any other professional class of women to experience mood disorders, drug addiction, panic attacks, eating disorders, and general anxiety disorder. They are also more likely to have experienced abuse during childhood. And as academics studying them, we were plunged into their stories of pain, despair, and suffering over and over and over again. It was just what you did in grad school. You read about women who went insane, and you wrote about women who went insane. And some of us went insane ourselves, writing about their insanity.

———

The alarm on my phone buzzes daily at eight a.m. It just says "P," but I know what this means. It's time to take Prozac. At night, I often need half an Ativan if it's been a panic-attack day, but I try not to take it unless I "feel like I am actually going to die," as my psychiatrist advises, because benzos have killed lots of writers. My sleep is infrequent and erratic, and my moods zip around unpredictably but mostly settle either in a zone of constant agitated worry or a lead blanket of a mood that presses me into inertia. I have wished, hoped, and many times prayed to simply turn my mind off, as much as I have been driven creatively and professionally by its wild expanses.

Unofficially, however, I'm just another crazy woman who writes.

The Catholic writer, poet, and civil rights activist Fanny Howe says that what being religious gives her is "an opportunity to examine one more completely insane vision of the universe."[3] She adds that the church, for all its obvious flaws, "has managed to accept the maddest among us," and "has a huge margin for visions." Whether a person believes in God or not, what all seekers have in common, according to Howe, is that sense that "to be saved only means to matter. You matter. Your life has meaning."

After abandoning religion in my teens when my father died and life felt gray and flat and devoid of meaning, I rediscovered Catholicism in my late thirties—yet another period when I did not feel like my life mattered. This cycle is familiar to people with major depressive disorder. Depression appears on the horizon in small ways, small personal stings that pile up, a few bad days at work, the news cycle, the pounds that pile on without you noticing them because your body is just a sack to be dragged around. And then, all of a sudden, there's a day when the full mass of depression presses down, an anvil of emotional pain, and the cycle begins again. Social withdrawal. A self-hatred so deeply rooted it can't be extricated from who you have become. Days that drag and nights that never end.

What religion offered was less a message of personal salvation and more a message that none of us, no matter how sick, angry, filthy, or unwanted, is truly alone. What faith gave me was a reminder that the ordinary world, even the world of depression, is still charged with grace. Gerard Manley Hopkins, the tubercular, closeted gay Victorian Jesuit who also suffered from depression himself, wrote that "the world is charged with the grandeur of God," full of "the dearest freshness deep down things."[4] That's what I found in Catholicism, as ill of a fit as it often was: it handed me an explanation for being in awe, a liturgical framework, a love for the poor, a link to my family history, and a community of saints, living and dead. But it could not take away my depression.

Anxiety, for those who've unfortunately experienced it, is more of a familiar, unwanted daily companion. It's always there, needling and prodding the mind to tumble into endless "what if" scenarios, all of them ending in catastrophe. People who live with overlapping anxiety and depression often feel guilty—so guilty, so repentant for things we have failed to do, so sinful, so unworthy.

We are, in other words, picture-perfect Catholics.

———

Here are some of the ways women through history have been treated for mental illness:

Lobotomy
Having holes drilled in their skulls (trepanning)
Burning at the stake/drowning/hanging
Bleeding and forced vomiting
Forced insulin coma
Injected with viruses to cause a fever to "burn out"
    hysteria
Unnecessary hysterectomy and oophorectomy
Ice-water baths
Physical restraints
Exorcism

Here are some side effects of medications taken for mental health today (just imagine this in the rapid voice-over of a TV advertisement): nausea, dry mouth, drowsiness, insomnia, lack of sexual desire, dizziness, weight loss, weight gain, indigestion, diarrhea, constipation, blurred vision, heavy sweating, hallucinations, seizures, suicidal thoughts.

These medications are what keep us alive.

———

Centuries before Simone Weil died from anorexia, Saint Catherine of Siena had a vision of her mystical marriage to Christ, during which he gave her a wedding ring made from his foreskin. Yes, that's correct. Many medieval saints received mystical rings in mystical weddings to Christ, and some of those saints were male (told you gender transgression is nothing new in religion), but only Catherine got a foreskin ring. She was that kind of special.

Catherine was one of those holy, mad women the church wasn't sure what to do with. When she fasted, she fasted to the point that she would only drink pus from the wounds of sick people (yes, it's gross; and yet another reason I wound up returning to Catholicism is probably because I'm fascinated by the grotesqueries of the human body, but also, Catholicism is very goth). When she spoke up to the men who led the church, she did so with a righteous anger that still resonates in her writing six centuries later. When her parents tried to stop her from becoming a nun, she shaved her head. God, according to Catherine, was the sea, and human beings were the fish. Her submission to God was extreme, even by the standards of her era. But was she mentally ill? By today's standards, absolutely. But this is more complicated when we look at the intersections of women, religious experience, and mental health.

In the times when they lived, mystics like Simone Weil, Julian of Norwich, Hildegard von Bingen, and Margery Kempe were understood to be vessels of God. Their visions came from God, the ability to translate those visions into prose or poetry or song came from God, and their deaths were things they fervently prayed for so that they would be united with God. If they suffered from madness, they understood this as God's will.

To most secular people and progressive religious people today, that kind of prayer can be disturbing. Do people really hear the voice of Jesus, feel God's touch, and understand that the Holy Spirit is moving among us? Yes, they do. But we no longer have folk saints like Christina the Astonishing, who arose out of her coffin at her own funeral in the twelfth century and flew up into the rafters because, it was said, she could smell the sin in the congregation. Christina, who we're told would also throw herself into furnaces, curl up into a ball on the ground and pretend to be a stone, and stand in frozen rivers for weeks on end, saw her actions (whether they were really this extreme or not) as a way of suffering on behalf of souls trapped in purgatory. Did she actually do these things? We can't know, but she *believed* she did them, and people who believed in her holiness looked past what others called madness and saw something else, something that might be closer to what might happen if a person really did hear the voice of God.

The problem is that today, the religious right has hijacked the conversation about how God talks to people. The language of white evangelicalism, particularly the politicized American version, rooted in its history of Calvinistic ideas of sin and predestination, emphasizes a person hearing Jesus or God speak to them not for the good of the community or the salvation of humankind like those mad women saints did, but for selfish, power-driven, and dangerous reasons.

The faith of prosperity-gospel preachers, gun-rights advocates making rosaries out of bullets, and "pro-life" men who assassinate doctors who perform abortions or plant bombs in clinics is, for many of us, what really feels like madness. Watching the increasingly tightly bound ties between nationalism and religion, white supremacy and religion, and homophobia/transphobia and religion and the stripping away of the health care mentally ill people rely on is like witnessing a collective episode of mental illness in light of what the gospels actually preach. If the purpose of religion is to make us better people, more concerned with others, and participants in the liberation of all of humanity, the religious right has foresworn belief in the opposite.

The hatred, suspicion, and fear of visionary women is real, too, including in the Catholic church, which has transformed its wild and untamable female saints into squeaky-clean, obedient, silent enigmas bereft of personality and representative of not much more than purity and piety. It is easier for religious or political institutions to point the finger and dismiss a woman as "crazy" than it is to unpack the overlapping social, cultural, and religious forces that exacerbate so many women's mental health issues in the first place. If those saints were just more crazy women littered throughout history, they're also easily erased.

———

Here are some things women were not allowed to do in 1971, the year I was born:

> Have a credit card in her own name
> Be guaranteed they could not be fired for getting pregnant
> Serve on a jury, depending on which state they lived in
> Fight in combat
> Go to Harvard, Brown, Dartmouth, or Columbia
> Report her husband for marital rape
> Pay the same amount for health insurance as a man
> Take birth control pills, depending on which state she lived in

Fifty years later, some things have changed for women in America. Certainly, we can at least be more vocal about issues, but fifty years after the Equal Rights Amendment (ERA) failed to be ratified, only half of the fifty states have equality amendments in their state constitutions. We have yet to elect a woman as president, and we still regularly tell and hear #MeToo stories. Women are statistically still more likely to be raped, abused, or killed by men than are men likely to be harmed by women. As I was writing this chapter, an older white, male member of Congress referred to a younger Latina female member of Congress as a "fucking bitch," was overheard saying it by a reporter, and refused to offer an apology. He in fact used his religious beliefs as an excuse for his "passion."[5]

The last I checked, Jesus never referred to a woman as a "fucking bitch." He did, however, minister to many women who were cast off by the society they lived in because of what would today be labeled mental illness. Mary Magdalene, wrongly described by men for centuries as a reformed prostitute, was actually someone from whom Jesus cast out demons, and in the time when this took place, people who were thought to be possessed by demons were often likely suffering from mental illness or some form of epilepsy. The woman who is hemorrhaging blood so badly during her periods that she actually tries to grab Jesus in order to be healed has visited doctor after doctor searching for solutions, wanting to be believed.

Today, when many women who present with symptoms of heart attacks and other life-threatening issues are brushed off by doctors as suffering from anxiety, the story of the woman with the hemorrhages might seem far too familiar. It's not unlikely that she, too, would be considered mentally ill by the same doctors. And if perhaps she is, that doesn't mean she shouldn't be listened to by medical professionals. For women, menopause, puberty, cancer treatments, and thyroid issues can throw off our biological chemistry so much that anxiety and depression are listed as side effects during treatment for any of those things. Take away the language we now have, the medications, the therapy, and the too-slow erasure of social stigmas around mental illness, and what you have left are suffering women no one listens to or believes. No wonder we were stigmatized as demonic, uncontrollable, possessed.

But in a Venn diagram between the holy madness of the saints and the ordinary madness of women, perhaps there is some overlap that's still relevant today, even with our sheaves of knowledge that former centuries lacked. Part of it is that we have not shaken off the stubborn yoke of patriarchy, which seeks to control women by labeling us as "crazy," whether that means we have something like bipolar disorder or are just having a bad day. What "crazy" means in a patriarchy is a woman who cannot be controlled, and a woman who cannot be controlled is ultimately a threat. That was true in the medieval era, and it remains so today.

After the medieval era, in the Renaissance, madness was the subject of both fascination and disgust. In Robert Burton's *Anatomy of Melancholy*, written in 1621, madness is not extraordinary but part of the everyday violence and shock of life, like much of what we experience today: "those ordinary rumours of war, plagues, fires, inundations, thefts, murders, massacres, meteors, comets, spectrums, prodigies, apparitions, of towns taken [and] cities besieged."[6]

In those same college English classes where I learned that all women who write will eventually go crazy, we also read a lot of Shakespeare and talked a lot about Ophelia. Ophelia—always handed to us as "poor Ophelia," the victim of an overbearing father, a terribly flaky and narcissistic boyfriend, a manipulative brother, and all of the expectations of sweetness and obedience that were piled onto teenage girls in her era. But like the medieval saints who came before her, Ophelia is also a visionary, a person possessed by ideas about guilt and shame that she may not actually be responsible for.

Ophelia's guilt, in other words, is a kind of religious guilt, guilt about sin and suffering that she shares with centuries of other women, which she takes on as a burden and which drags her down to her death. The medieval saints who preceded her believed their ailments were miracles sent from God. Ophelia gets one "mad scene" onstage, but her death occurs offstage, a footnote in a man's story. And the other mad women and girls of literature, from Anna Karenina to Madame Bovary, from Jane Eyre's "woman in the attic" to the authors of the landslide of memoirs about women's mental illness in the late twentieth century, had to combat that same guilt and shame, and are still struggling to throw it off even today.

Literature and religion may have shaped my view of madness, but when seven women are disabled by depression for every man who experiences the same thing,[7] we are not just talking about religious-leaning women or women writers being caged by centuries of social stigma. We are talking about women in every occupation, in every part of the world, who are considered to be crazy. It might be easy to say that we are past the point when women who were mentally ill were killed or encouraged to kill themselves, that our world is more civilized, more aware. But this is not the case. At all.

In 2015, Sandra Bland, a twenty-eight-year-old Black activist, was pulled over by Texas state trooper Brian Encinia for failing to use her turn signal. He yanked her out of the car, threw her to the ground, and took her to jail, where she hanged herself. Bland, who seems to have struggled with depression, was not placed on suicide watch in prison, and the FBI later found that the guards were not adequately trained in working with mentally ill people. Her family said she had recently been excited about a new job, but friends also talked about Bland's ups and downs, and some of her downs were apparently dire. Based on what she told a prison guard, she had been "very depressed" for the past year.[8] It was clear that she needed help. She got nothing.

Following her death, her family eventually settled a wrongful-death suit, and the Sandra Bland Act went into effect in 2017. The act requires jails to collect information to determine if a person is mentally ill. Whatever the truth was about Sandra Bland's mental health, from the cop who arrested her to the wardens where she was incarcerated to the media afterward, she was portrayed as a woman who was crazy, and that image was used to explain her suicide, when in fact it's not unlikely that violent and racist treatment at the hands of police played an outsized part in the premature end of her life. What if Sandra Bland was mentally ill and died because of it, or because law enforcement officers didn't know how to deal with mental illness? What if she wasn't mentally ill, and she died because cops and wardens thought she was?

Perhaps Sandra Bland is a better patron saint for the mentally ill than Dymphna. Or we could choose Carrie Fisher, who harnessed her bipolar disorder into a career as an actor and writer, or Billie Holiday, whose addictions were a side effect of the racism and sexism she also experienced, or the painter Jay DeFeo, who dealt with anxiety and depression as one of the few abstract expressionist women artists in a very macho art world, or even Mother Teresa, who spent decades sunk deep into depression, hiding it from public view the entire time. We can choose from so many women who heard what the saints called the voice of God and what doctors now call mental illness and channeled it into care for others, creative life, deep empathy, and transformative compassion. And we can understand that the threat posed by mentally ill women is the same threat posed by any woman who listens to her own mind.

———

When I began thinking in the framework of faith and madness and the expectations piled on women, I thought again about Sylvia Plath and what she stands for, and about "Lady Lazarus," Plath's poem about her suicide attempts and the persistence of her desire to bring an end to her suffering. Lazarus, so beloved of Jesus that he was raised from the dead, never has the opportunity to tell us what that felt like, or whether he even wanted to come back, so Plath tells us. It "feels like hell." And the survivor of madness that she becomes is not a waifish ghost like Ophelia, or an elliptical mystery like Simone Weil, or able to survive on the eucharist alone like Catherine of Siena. The communion Plath takes becomes an act of devouring her own suffering and using it to set the world around her on fire. "Out of the ash," she writes, "I rise with my red hair / and I eat men like air."[9]

FOUR

BARREN

Three religions were born in deserts: Christianity, Judaism, and Islam. In each of these religions, God is portrayed in language of the masculine. The desert, in these religious imaginations, is barren—bereft of life—until Allah/Yahweh/God rains down manna, water, the Holy Spirit, and infuses the land and nourishes the people with life. Even though the world's deserts actually teem with forms of life and are homes to millions of people indigenous to those landscapes, this idea of barrenness as empty lifelessness remains entrenched in the collective imagination. What has been the basis of our religious imagination in the West is the image of barren land and a barren people that can only be infused with life by . . . a masculine God.

Talk about heteronormativity.

Talk about how this definition of barrenness has shaped our collective imagination.

These masculine ways of imagining this specific landscape and the God of that landscape are reflective of the human violence of history. But in these desert religions, too, there is an often-suppressed feminine imagination present—feminine in the sense of Sophia, of the divine feminine. Perhaps we are now, in the early twenty-first century, at a turning point, with women rabbis and women Christian pastors and priests and women Muslim spiritual leaders who are hardly subservient, who are reclaiming those texts of the desert, and the desert itself with its life-giving properties as a place of the feminine wisdom of Sophia.

The masculine language of "barrenness" for land-scapes, and for women who are unable or who choose not to give birth, is pinned not only to the metaphors in religion that speak to spiritual understandings, but also to our physical bodies in the very way we mark the eras of a woman's life as either fertile or not. Western culture has cast barrenness as punishment, as failure, as a mistake, as nongrowth. In this vision, barrenness is the landscape and our bodies at the same time—until someone or something else arrives and changes that. In that construct, perhaps God. Perhaps a man.

Perhaps that, too, is what needs to change.

———

It wasn't until I was in my forties that I started getting asked to travel places and speak. No matter where I go, and no matter who I speak to, one of the questions is inevitably the same. A lovely, tiny older woman in Cleveland asks it. A loud-talking, bearded guy in New York asks it. A shy woman from Africa asks it in Rome. A college student asks it at pretty much every college. I talk to a lot of religious groups, so nuns ask it, priests ask it, and pastors ask it. Once I sat next to a bishop at a formal dinner and he asked it. I don't give talks on the subject. It has nothing to do with most of my writing and research. And yet, someone always has to ask. Someone always thinks it's their business.

"Do you have children?"

When my uterus was sliced into ribbons and tugged out of my body, it had never fulfilled its biological purpose but had instead given me decades of heavy bleeding and pain. Could it have sheltered a baby? I only know that it never did, and whatever emotional negotiations I had to make about that were over and done with by the time it was removed. My surgeon told me that any odds of getting pregnant at forty-eight were so minuscule and rife with danger and expense, my equipment wasn't even worth consideration. "If you're not using it, let's just take it all out," was her motto.

Regrets—I only had a few.

And yet, people continue to be insatiably curious about my reproductive capacity, and that curiosity has not faded even as I have passed into the postreproductive era. Do I have children? Reader, I do not, and I have yet to work up a snappy comeback to that question along the lines of what Rebecca Solnit asks of her interlocutors: "Would you ask a man that?" A response that tells us that asking a woman if she has children is "indecent, because it presumed that women should have children, and that a woman's reproductive activities were naturally public business. More fundamentally," Solnit adds, "the question assumed that there was only one proper way for a woman to live."[1]

What I have yet to figure out is why people care. In 2020, the American birth rate is at an all-time low. By the time women reach their late forties, 15 percent of us have never had children, and higher numbers of millennial and Gen Z women than any generation before say that having children is not a priority for them. In my liberal bubble of a 1970s Bay Area childhood, it was still pretty taboo to say that you didn't think you wanted to be a mom; today, young women are much more frank about it—and about the fact that with the financial and career challenges stacked against them, they'd rather keep putting off the decision anyway. Yet, people just keep asking.

Barrenness is fixated in the Western imagination as a kind of dualistic failure. On the one hand, the woman has not reproduced, and civilization itself could be at risk. That is the same failure of imagination that sees desert landscapes only as lifeless. Consider the P. D. James novel *The Children of Men*, where barrenness is global as the result of human behavior, and the life of the one viably pregnant woman on earth must be protected at all costs. Rather than realizing that like every other species, humankind is inevitably going to expire, a single pregnancy becomes the fragile hope humanity is pinned to, even as humanity is depicted as being completely self-destructive.

On that last note, fail #2: Contemplating barrenness in the time of accelerating climate change is loaded with dangers. The planet itself is becoming barren—the entire planet, not just the land but the water and sky. But the pace of births means that even as crops fail and species vanish, those babies will need food and clean water and skies that won't allow the sun's rays to fry their skin. The planet is losing its capacity to provide those things.

And yet, when a woman doesn't reproduce for whatever reason, even in the face of global catastrophe, she is still considered a failure. And in spite of that, many countries still don't offer families much in the way of a social safety net, meaning that we both push women into motherhood and then fail to support mothers.

But the question remains: Why is our fertility anyone's business? At some level this might be just simple curiosity and a desire to make small talk. People with kids like talking about their kids, and that's easier to do with other people who have kids. This is why the spinster aunt doesn't get invited, and this is why women without kids have radar for one another: because we're not at the toddler bacchanal or whatever event all the parents went to. *Oh, you're not at the toddler bacchanal either? You must also be barren. Huzzah! Pull up a chair.*

The childless are always, in other words, being outed. "Do you have children?" is an easy question to ask if you have children because the assumption is that everyone else does. But it's also unfair and deeply problematic, like greeting someone by saying, "Did you lose weight?" only to find out they have cancer or just got out of a psychiatric hospital or were recently divorced. Solnit notes that interlocutors about her fertility seem to usually be men, but women are guilty of this as well, maybe even more so.

There is also the problem that for some women, not having children feels like a space of deep regret and loss, and those questions are painful and wounding. For other women, the maternal instinct is simply absent and is not something they grieve lacking, yet they too are judged and condemned. And there are the many women who hover somewhere in between, who experience a profoundly complex set of emotions about not having children. But all of them are trapped by the same idea: that they have somehow failed.

In some cases, a woman moving beyond the idea that barrenness is failure means she must deconstruct or reinvent the idea of family. For others, it means an opportunity to better understand the self and to forge a vocation. And for others, it means living so far outside the box that a new box must be created. There are as many ways to be childless as there are women without children—a number that increases all the time. But the important thing is that we need to stop defining those women by the idea of their lives as a perpetual state of absence.

In a world where reproductivity is one of the ways we define normativity for women, barrenness and being without children is a signal of something potentially dangerous. And for those of us without children, many are still bracing and cringing in anticipation of the question because it always, always, always gets asked. Add *Catholic* to that equation, and you immediately bring a couple more *alwayses* to the probability.

———

In the Hebrew Bible, fertility is seen by the Israelites as a gift from God, and the lack of it as God's punishment.

"Biblical women who experience periods of barrenness often understand their inability to conceive as a divine withholding of blessing, a punishment, or even a curse," writes Cynthia Chapman.[2] For women in the Hebrew Bible, fertility is a divinely endowed gift, and not having children means the curse of separation from the tribe. Scripture relates that Michal, the daughter of Saul, "had no child to the day of her death" (2 Samuel 6:23), and the prophet Hosea tells us that the punishment that God will lay on the nation of Ephraim (Israel) is "no birth, no pregnancy, no conception" (Hosea 9:11).

But just as the Israelites' desert landscape, where Sophia abides, reveals feminine wisdom, we begin to understand that this is only one side of the narrative. Digging deeper into the Hebrew Bible, Miriam, Judith, the midwives Shiphrah and Puah, Dinah, the daughters of Zelophehad, Deborah, Jael, Vashti, and Esther are all either childless or their children are not mentioned, which is significant in scriptures so concerned with lineage. If their children aren't mentioned, it may well be that they didn't have any. In the New Testament, Anna the prophetess, Mary and Martha of Bethany, and many of the women in the early church like Tabitha, Lydia, Junia, and Phoebe, as well as Thecla from the apocryphal Acts of Paul and Thecla, are never mentioned as being mothers. And again, this is in books so obsessed with lineage that Jesus's family tree is regularly trotted out for emphasis. Jesus and Paul, of course, never had children either, according to the texts, but the church fathers don't dwell on that, probably figuring they were so busy that they wouldn't have been great at diaper changing.

Among the mentions of childless women in the Hebrew Scriptures and New Testament, some stand out, both because of their strength of character and because they became leaders of their people. Vashti, the first wife of Persian king Ahasuerus, is herself childless and refuses to be paraded before his dinner guests, so the king replaces her with Esther, who is secretly Jewish. Esther's cousin Mordecai offends the king's adviser Haman, so Haman asks permission to kill all the Jews in Persia. Esther throws a wrench into his plans by revealing Haman's plot to the king and by revealing that she, too, is Jewish. Haman gets executed, and the Jewish people of Persia are granted the right to defend themselves against their enemies. On Purim, the Scroll of Esther is read in synagogues as Jewish people celebrate their delivery from annihilation at Haman's hands.

Growing up Catholic, I knew almost nothing about Esther's story—it's often buried in the daily readings for church services, and very few Catholics attend church on weekdays and hear those readings. And it's probably not coincidental that since Catholicism emphasizes the role of women as wives and mothers more than anything else, these stories of childless women in the Bible were muted at best, erased at worst.

But when my sister converted to Judaism, I began to learn more about these strong women in the Hebrew

Scriptures. Discovering that a pivotal figure like Esther, who saves her people from death, also happens to be childless helped me see that reading childlessness as a curse in these books is, in fact, incorrect. For some of these women, the curse ends when God "opens their womb," but for others, their childless state is simply never mentioned, yet they are honored and celebrated as heroic figures, prophetesses, and deliverers of their people. In Isaiah, the prophet commands barren women to sing because "the children of the desolate woman will be more than the children of her that is married" (Isaiah 54:1).

If we don't take this literally, because so much in the Bible simply cannot be taken literally, we might consider it figuratively instead. Perhaps Esther never had children, but the Jewish people of Persia, saved by her quick thinking, still revered her as a leader and so are considered her "children."

And Miriam, the sister of Moses and one of the major prophetesses, is associated with Miriam's Well, a miraculous spring that kept the Israelites alive during the exodus. Since the 1980s, Jewish feminists have added a cup of water to the seder table to celebrate Miriam's *mayyim hayyim*—the same "living water" Jesus will later drink from when it is handed to him by a woman, also at a well. Letty Cottin Pogrebin says that for Jewish women, Miriam, who led her people through the parted waters of the Red Sea by singing and dancing, "introduced the notion of radical change as worthy of celebration."[3] And in a subversion of role and identification, unlike with her brother Moses, the text never mentions whether or not Miriam had children.

In the New Testament, Jesus unexpectedly first appears after his resurrection not to the band of male followers, but to a Jewish woman, Mary Magdalene (John 20:1–10). It is she who runs and tells the male apostles what she's seen. They, of course, don't believe her, which not only makes her the patron saint of mansplaining, but also means that the first person to proclaim the resurrection is a single, childless woman. She was, effectively, a priest. Like Esther and Miriam, if Mary Magdalene ever had children, they aren't mentioned, and that frees her up not only to be an apostle, but to build a relationship with Jesus that's so profound and trusting that he's willing to choose her over the men who followed him. Their relationship has been imagined by many writers, mostly male, from Nikos Kazantzakis to Dan Brown, as carnal, rather than platonic, because what could two childless people get up to other than sex and reproduction?

Feminist theologians would rather meet Mary Magdalene as she arrives: alone, unencumbered, and ready to reinvent herself. In Saint-Maximin-la-Sainte-Baume, France, there is a shrine purporting to be her last resting place, because according to local lore, she arrived there in a boat without oars or sails, later to spend her days in a cave, ministering to those who managed to find her. What the patriarchal tradition taught us instead, with no evidence, is that she was a repentant prostitute whose only option was to seek forgiveness from a man. Imagine if we'd learned, instead, that she arrived of her own volition, shaped her own reinvention, and led her community through dangerous times. Imagine what contemporary religion might look like.

———

If we want to reimagine barrenness, we also have to consider that self-forged ties can be as tightly bound and as nurturing as familial ones. A person may not have biological children, may not have adopted children, but can create ties of friendship and community that can help lead us to new understandings of what it means to care for one another.

With divorces having peaked in America in the 1970s, many Gen Xers, millennials, and Gen Zers grew up in blended families or single-parent households. For the queer community, this reinvention of family became more mainstream along with their slow but steady march toward greater social acceptance. It's not uncommon today to see TV shows and films featuring same-sex parenting couples, and in most parts of the country, there are fewer hurdles to LGBTQ couples adopting or using fertility clinics than there were in the recent past.

However, queer parents are still *parents*. Even more radical models for queer families have existed outside the gaze of straight society for a very long time. Before same-sex marriage was legalized and LGBTQ parents received adoption protections from the Supreme Court, many Americans learned about self-invented queer families not from the pages of the *New York Times* or from the newest Netflix show, but from a newspaper serial written by a gay man in San Francisco.

In 1978, Armistead Maupin began writing *Tales of the City* for the *San Francisco Chronicle*. Maupin's biography reads like the life story of one of his fictional characters. Raised in the South, he worked for a TV station owned by the ultraconservative senator Jesse Helms, and it wasn't until Maupin moved to San Francisco in 1971 that he went from being a closeted Republican to a very out gay progressive. Maupin had a front-row seat to the gay rights movement as it grew and flourished, particularly around San Francisco's Castro neighborhood, where he still lives. But he also had a wicked sense of humor and a big, soft heart for his eclectic, endearingly flawed characters in *Tales*. Some were loosely based on real people, some were barely fictionalized versions of local celebrities (including the flamingly gay celebrity Catholic priest who hosts a TV chat show called *Honest to God*), and some were based on various aspects of Maupin's own personality and experiences. The serial blended fiction and fact and ran for many years before it spun off into multiple books and three TV series.

The beating heart of *Tales*, however, is Anna Madrigal. The landlady of the ramshackle house on fictional Barbary Lane, Madrigal is a bit of a cipher when the characters first encounter her. Initially, she seems like the kind of pot-smoking kooky old broad in a kimono who's pretty much been priced out of San Francisco for good in the wake of gentrification. But it's not long before Maupin reveals her not-so-secret secret, which cements her role as a queer icon. Anna Madrigal is trans, one of the first people to undergo a surgical transition, and she doesn't bother to hide this: her name is a self-chosen anagram of "A Man and A Girl."

Anna is beloved by the tenants in her apartment building, both gay and straight, and as the series go on, that core group of characters grows to include a younger generation of trans characters, who see her as a mentor. Madrigal often refers to her tenants and ex-tenants as her "logical family" as opposed to her biological one.

In Maupin's universe, family cannot be confined to couples with children. Even if some couples in the *Tales* saga do have kids, Maupin always brings the focus back to that idea of "logical" family. For queer people whose own biological families may have rejected them or pushed them away, finding Anna means they have found the nurturing and acceptance they lacked. As a young adult, I devoured these books when I saw in them the potential for both self-reinvention and a richly rewarding life spent caring for others outside the confines of heteronormative roles. Outside the confines of roles. Outside the patriarchy definitions of *barren* and *fecund*. Outside that idea of deserts as lifeless places. As an adult without children, I have returned to these books many times, a kind of literary comfort food, because I love the way Maupin tells a bigger story about words, terms, and roles that have been historically limited, and shows that we don't have to regenerate to model regenerative love.

In the Catholic church, the views of women without children are multidimensional and also often self-contradictory. The church praises women with children and encourages them to have as many as possible, but it also praises women religious, sisters and nuns, who largely do not have children because they take vows of chastity and live a celibate life, although there are rare exceptions of widows with kids who join these orders. But even while these communities of women are still attached to a patriarchal institutional church, a few among them have constructed a more horizonal version of leadership, one in which decisions are made only after many rounds of conversation and discernment about the common good of the group. Because they don't have children, these nuns and sisters can reconceptualize the way their communities function rather than adhering to the same top-down structure as the rest of the church, which is the very reason the Vatican chose to investigate them in 2012 for espousing "radical feminist themes."

The stereotype of the knuckle-cracking sister in a habit tormenting elementary school kids is pretty much a relic of the pre-Vatican II era. Since then, as their numbers have contracted, some women religious have taken greater risks instead of shrugging in surrender: speaking out on social justice issues, showing up at demonstrations, working with LGBTQ Catholics, even putting their lives on the line in dangerous parts of the world, and sometimes, like the four Maryknoll Sisters who died in El Salvador in 1980, being murdered because of their social activism.

Until the mid-twentieth century, and in some parts of the world even today, making the deliberate choice to give up marriage and children was sometimes a way for Catholic sisters to protect themselves from arranged marriages, rape, domineering fathers, and every other element of a patriarchal society that makes women's lives hell. Today, because the choice to become a sister is increasingly rare, it is also increasingly countercultural. In a nation that sends women so many mixed messages about sex (have it for yourself, but mostly, have it to keep men happy), sisters say "no, thanks" to that negotiation. They say no to being biological mothers in a culture that also tells women that not being a mother is a failure, and yet, many of them I know work harder than anyone teaching, counseling, nursing, lawyering, writing, advocating, and loving the broken world we live in. They grow into their own agency.

——

The average woman with two ovaries is born with a million eggs. They are already dying before we can even begin to use them. By the time she reaches puberty, only three hundred thousand are left. In her lifetime, only five hundred will ovulate, and the remainder will die off at menopause. Even the most fecund woman could never produce five hundred offspring, a biblical number at best, a global catastrophe if it were even remotely possible at worst. That some religions have reduced women's value to their reproductive worth has become one of the many reasons increasing numbers of younger women have lost interest in participating in religion. And the more we have also learned about the spectrum of gender identities, the less the idea of women being defined by their fertility or lack thereof makes sense.

What's more, there are as many kinds of mothers as there are women without children. When we reduce motherhood to a kind of pious simplicity, an unstoppable font of goodness, we also ignore all the complexities that come with having children and turn motherhood into a series of hollow clichés. While I may not have many regrets about not being a mother, it still feels like a betrayal when my church invites mothers up to the altar on Mother's Day to receive flowers, while the rest of us are left sitting in our pews, revealed to everyone as childless, which is, frankly, nobody's business. Imagine how much more painful that experience is for the woman struggling with infertility, the woman with ovarian cancer, or the woman whose child has died, perhaps violently. When we criticize women for not having children, we also pit women against one another, reduce them to "good" versus "bad," when, in fact, the moral and ethical and psychological complexities all women have to negotiate are not solely determined by their ability to procreate.

The desert faiths have missed out on the complexities of women's lives in the same ways people who look at a desert and see lifelessness have missed the genius of creation that allows cacti to store water in their leaves, gives people the vision of building their homes in the side of cave walls, helps every kind of crawling and leaping thing to adapt. The notion that women in Scripture are mothers or nothing is also an erasure of quite a lot of extraordinary women, their stories buried over time.

Like everything alive in the desert, women who live without children adapt and survive. Sometimes it strikes me that this is what Sophia also had to do. She is also the Shekinah, who rabbinical literature tells us is the dwelling place of God. Perhaps she is Guan Yin, the bodhisattva of compassion, or Hoo-soo'-pe, the Miwok water maidens, sisters of Wek'-wek, the falcon who brings people into the world. Sophia could be Mary Magdalene, or the Samaritan woman Jesus meets at the well, whom Eastern Rite Christians call Saint Photini. Or she could be living in the wild Celtic landscapes called "thin places," in the towering redwoods, in the sea, and yes, in the deserts. Or she's any woman, hewing her own path, trying to re-create herself when others have looked at her and seen only emptiness, have dismissed her or given up on her as a failure of fecundity. This is the unexpected second bloom, the surprise spring of water, the stranger appearing, walking on the heat-shimmering road. The woman, emerging, on her own.

FIVE

BUTCH/ FEMME/ OTHER

Women's lives in the Middle Ages were dirty and short. While still in your early teens, you were either pregnant and in danger of dying in childbirth or sent off to a drafty, perpetually damp convent where you weren't allowed to wear shoes and your hair was hacked off, so you were likely to frequently be sick with colds, flu, or pneumonia, any of which could kill you. No matter where you lived, you either died from plagues or you survived them, but the latter was mostly luck because doctors treated most illnesses by slicing people's arms and bleeding them. There was almost nothing in the way of recourse if something violent happened to you, other than inciting or enduring more violence.

Your teeth could kill you. Your uterus could kill you. The cut the doctor made on your arm with a dirty knife could kill you. Your husband could kill you, and so could your father, and no one really cared if they did.

Considering the ways in which women's lives were flung so far out of their control, the legend of the medieval Saint Wilgefortis represents a defiance against that lack of control. But it also tends to be filed by most people under "Catholic Weird."

The story of Wilgefortis began not with a specific woman, but with a piece of art, not of Wilgefortis, but of Jesus. Medieval images of Jesus on the cross sometimes showed him clad in a full-length androgynous tunic instead of the loincloth most of us are more familiar with, and as these pieces of art traveled around Europe, they took flight in the vivid, pious medieval imagination and sometimes merged with other narratives. Here's how one narrative was born.

Once upon a time, a young noblewoman named Wilgefortis was promised to a man in marriage by her father. Christians of the medieval era were terrified of Muslims, who they believed to be infidels due both to their own ignorance of Islam and to teachings from Rome, so the legend was spun for maximum stir-fear-into-the-hearts-of-believers effect. Thus, the man to whom Wilgefortis was promised was a Muslim king. Wilgefortis, a good virgin girl, began praying that she would become disgusting so the king would refuse her, and in answer to her prayers, God helped her to grow a long, prominent beard. The king lost interest, and the girl's father had her crucified. She died. The end.

Or . . . maybe not. As it turns out, like a few other saints of her era, Wilgefortis wasn't real, and within a couple hundred years, the story's origins started to be questioned. Because the notion of an androgynous Christ figure wasn't entirely unheard-of in the Middle Ages, its adoption into the story of Wilgefortis isn't as weird as may appear. And as her story traveled the world, devotions to her only grew. In England, she was called Uncumber, and in Italy she was known as Liberata. Her miraculous beard, and its ability to help Wilgefortis avoid an undesired marriage, was a medieval version of feminism.

To return to Wilgefortis's forerunners, in some medieval images of the suffering Christ, the wounds on his body look almost exactly like a vulva. In other images, he has breasts, and medieval devotions often refer to the blood of Christ as being like mother's milk. As the Middle Ages marched on, the anima, or the soul, increasingly began to be referred to as female. Feminism and subversion of roles march in and through that era too. Women who wrote devotional literature at the time sometimes referred to themselves as men, and male monks sometimes referred to themselves as women. Julian of Norwich, a woman who took a man's name, wrote of God and Christ as mother figures. Medieval women disguised themselves as men to enter monasteries.

In other words, while the default image of God in the Middle Ages was male, the religious imagination of the time was far more expansive than the idea of gender as binary might suggest.

———

When we use the word *women* today, what do we mean? The question has become much more complicated—and much more interesting—since people began to talk about the differences between sex and gender, and about the differences between bodies and minds, between how we are born and how we identify ourselves. As long as gender has existed, gender transgressors have existed. Aside from the fact that some people are born with penises and testicles and some people are born with ovaries and uteruses and some are born with combinations of these, we have been busily trying to untangle biological distinctions related to how we think, act, and feel for thousands of years.

When I refer to women, I am talking about people who identify as women, meaning *all women*. It would be relatively easy for someone to decide that since I no longer have a uterus or functioning ovaries, I don't make enough estrogen to be a woman, and as I don't take estrogen supplements, that same someone may decide my chemical makeup is neither male nor female but a kind of undulating genetic slush. In *Flash Count Diary*, Darcey Steinke writes that postmenopausal women enter a liminal space, a postgendered space.[1]

As a child I had short hair and dressed like a boy, and when people complimented my father on his son, he did not bother to correct them. I think about being at the Baseball Hall of Fame in Cooperstown, New York, with my dad and hearing someone say, "How nice of you to bring your son all the way here," and taking stock of my prepubescent body, wondering, *What is this, anyway?* And I think about how my body has changed more recently and see the scars where my uterus came out and wonder now, about my menopausal body, *What is this, anyway?* Frankly, I don't think about my body much until some part of it hurts or, as with the Cooperstown comment, gets pointed out, and that's a privilege.

My mind matches my body, for the most part, and thus I'm a woman in the cisgender sense. I've also known many women who are women in the transgender sense, in that their minds and bodies did not match until they made a few adjustments. They are women, too, because every woman makes adjustments and accommodations. That's what I mean when I say "women." I mean all of us—thinking, accommodating, matching.

But then we get to Wilgefortis. Whether Wilgefortis was real or not is mostly irrelevant; what matters is that people loved Wilgefortis. They loved the idea that a woman could be liberated from her father by becoming like a man. They also loved Joan of Arc, who wore men's clothing, and they loved Saint Euphrosyne, who transformed herself into a monk named Smaragdus and lived for thirty-eight years in the monastery as a man, never discovered until they died. They loved Saint Hildegonde, who became a Trappist named "Brother Joseph," and they loved Saint Francis's friend Jacoba, whom Francis called "Brother" as well. In the Orthodox church they venerate Anastasia the Patrician, who lived as a desert hermit for decades in the 500s BCE, in a time when only men were allowed to be hermits, and they loved dozens and dozens of other gender-transgressing saints and holy people.

Medieval people painted images of Jesus giving birth through the wound in his side, and they painted images of massive vulvas in the margins of manuscripts, and they queered Christianity before they even understood what queering something meant.

The wild imagination of the early Christian church was trampled down eventually, into "complementarianism" and the notion that gender is binary, fixed, and unchangeable, even as science and psychology and our own minds and the changes taking place within our own bodies tell us differently. And out of that mindset came conversion therapy, high suicide rates, self-harm, and addiction for many kids from Christian families who struggled to live within those binary boundaries. Not until very recently have trans and openly queer people been able to be ordained in a relatively small number of Christian denominations, and in many other Christian denominations, they continue to be muted and hidden away or shamed out of existence. Catholic tradition, once venerating the same, has somehow also managed to try to erase that part of its history.

When we talk about women, and how women don't fit in, we need to talk about the transgression beyond binary gender, because that is both a very old idea and one that increasingly looks like the future.

Because how we understand women needs to change, how we understand gender needs to change as well.

———

Before we can begin to understand what *gender* means in a context that includes spirituality and religion, we also have to understand the ways in which gender has been misunderstood in the Venn diagram of those overlapping contexts. As a person from a Catholic background, I can only speak to my own tradition with any kind of expertise, but there are long-standing problems in our general Judeo-Christian understanding of gender and God.

Primarily, the idea that God is male is not necessarily scripturally correct. Hebrew Bible scholar Gina Hens-Piazza tells us this is rooted in language. "Hebrew pronouns," she writes, "don't always compute with our concept of gender."[2] Thus the language of identifying Israel with an abused woman, or the Catholic church referring to itself as female even while it only ordains men, means an objectification of women when "objectification is not the work of women, but of those that have power [over women]."

As far back as the seventeenth century, Baruch Spinoza questioned the idea of assigning a gender to God, because thinking of God as a gendered being meant thinking of God as corporeal, a view that led to Spinoza being excommunicated from the Talmud Torah congregation of Amsterdam. But later, male Jewish thinkers from Martin Buber to Mordecai Kaplan to Zalman Schachter-Shalomi would agree with Spinoza and move to the position that God cannot be gendered because God is an experience, a relationship, or a process.

In the New Testament, Jesus is born as a man most likely because in the context of the time, God understood that a woman would not have held the authority a male Jesus could, or she would not have been seen as a rabbinical figure capable of leading a community. The culture of Jesus's era was androcentric, and women were typically relegated to supporting roles. Even so, Jesus defied masculine stereotypes in more ways than one.

His first public miracle, transforming water into wine, came at the prompting of his mother, who herself moved beyond gender norms if you believe in the concept of the immaculate conception. Mary is the *theotokos*, the God-bearer: she literally holds God in her body and gives birth to God, a God whose father is also God and whose father is also a spirit whose gender is probably female: the Hebrew word for "spirit" is *ruach*, which is feminine. That same spirit is also known as Sophia, the Sophia mentioned earlier who is a feminine embodiment of God. So a woman is impregnated by a woman-gendered spirit who was sent by a genderless God. You can also add in Saint Joseph, Jesus's human stepfather, and Jesus's unnamed but very much present tribe of brothers and sisters, whose parentage is unclear. Needless to say, Jesus does not exactly come from standard societal definitions of anything, including that of a "nuclear family."

As an adult, Jesus continued to break through cultural, social, and gender norms. He healed anyone who needed to be healed, regardless of their gender or social status. He shared water with the Samaritan woman at the well—not only a woman but a member of a marginalized minority group—and sent her forth to be the first witness to his ministry. Then, as we've discussed, after his resurrection, the first person he appeared to was also a woman. When he knelt and washed the feet of his disciples at the Last Supper, Jesus took on the position of a woman, who would normally have been the one to perform that action. Women were the last ones at the foot of the cross when Jesus died, were among the leaders of the early church after his ascension, and traveled to spread his message. His followers were a discipleship of equals. All of this not only makes the continuing resistance to women's ordination in some denominations an absurdity, it also points out that the people who created Christianity often had more radical ideas about gender than the simplistic notions the church trumpets today.

Prophecy, throughout history, has usually had a gender. Jews and Christians have a variety of prophets depicted in the Bible, mostly male, but a handful of female prophetic voices are tossed in as well: Miriam, Deborah, Huldah, Anna, Mary the mother of Jesus, Mary Magdalene. In American Christianity, however, faith has been influenced by Puritan and Calvinist ideologies about sin and predestination that have punished women for stepping out of assigned gender norms. The witch hunts and slut-shaming and policing of female bodies and sexuality and the emphasis on female bodies as vessels for reproduction and not much else inherent in American Christian history have meant that in this country, women were not encouraged to be prophetic. Most denominations in America didn't even start ordaining women until late in the twentieth century, and even those that do still grapple with sexist, patriarchal structures and thinking.

Of course, there are a few exceptions. The Shakers, founded by the visionary Mother Ann Lee, were an eighteenth-century American religious community that believed Lee was the second coming of Christ in female form. Lee was so worried about sin and temptation among her followers that she not only separated men and women in Shaker communities but also made celibacy a requirement for joining the Shakers, part of the reason their numbers dwindled rapidly after an initial surge in interest. While we mostly know Shakers today from their simple but elegant designs for furniture and home-building, they did elevate women to equal leadership roles in a time when that was strikingly unlikely.

About a hundred years after Ann Lee, Mary Baker Eddy, a spiritualist who believed that prayer could overcome any bodily injury or illness, founded the Christian Science movement, which is still extant today. Eddy's spirituality can seem dated and antiquated to many skeptical about Christian Science's denial of the efficacy of modern medicine, but in her lifetime and after, she contributed to the rapid growth of a truly American religious movement. Later, women like Dorothy Day and Fannie Lou Hamer would prove to be prophetic about the links between faith and action on behalf of the poor and of Black Americans. But all of these women prophets were still women.

There was one American religious prophet who began life as a woman, but ended it as someone genderless, and new.

In the year 1776, America was transformed in more ways than one. Not only did it become a nation independent of Britain, but it also witnessed the birth of the Public Universal Friend, in their own way as unexpected and transformative as the idea of America itself. Born in a kind of egalitarian optimism scarred by the legacy of the slaves they owned, the founders' vision of America was one in which the First Amendment declared that America would neither have a national religion nor prohibit worship in any religion. Religion, Thomas Jefferson wrote, is "a matter that lies solely between Man & his God."[3] For the Public Universal Friend, that might be better phrased as "Man & their God."

In 1776 Jemima Wilkinson, a twenty-three-year-old Quaker, was bedridden with a fever. Like many prophets, Jemima's illness was the moment of transformation, from a young Quaker woman into a genderless figure self-dubbed the Public Universal Friend.[4] The Friend confounded people in the eighteenth century by dressing in the garb of a male cleric, but with women's shoes. The Friend's hair was worn like a man's wig of the era in front and long and curly in the back. The followers of the Friend used male pronouns to refer to the resurrected Friend, and usually used female pronouns to refer to the Friend's past life as Jemima. The Friend's detractors—and there were many—always referred to the Friend as she.

The pre-Revolutionary War period in America was extremely unstable and fraught with unknowns. The religious marketplace was suddenly flung wide open as the colonists rejected the Church of England and began to foment their own religious movements, along with exploring imported denominations like Methodism and The Society of Friends, better known as the Quakers. Just a few decades after the arrival of the Public Universal Friend and not that far from the Universal Friends' colony in New York, Joseph Smith would publish the Book of Mormon. In the religious landscape of early America, a charismatic leader like the Friend or Smith could easily attract followers because early Americans had so much to fear: war, disease, hunger, early death.

The Friend was almost never born. When Jemima Wilkinson succumbed to a fever, she had already been visiting experimental and charismatic religious communities outside her family's Quaker one and, it seems, was likely mentally combining them together into her own ideological theology. When Jemima recovered from that sickness and rose from her sickbed, she told her family it was time for her "to assume the body which God has prepared for the spirit to dwell in."[5] That body was the body of the Public Universal Friend. According to the Friend, that body did not have a gender.

The Friend's preaching career was a challenge. Women were not supposed to preach in public in the Friend's era, but because of the Friend's androgyny, the crowds attracted to the Friend were not always sure what gender the Friend really was. The beliefs the Friend and their followers preached were also fairly radical for the time; they were abolitionists who believed in universal equality. Several members of the Universal Friends were Black, about four dozen of them were unmarried women who took on preaching and ministry roles, and they lived a simple, communal lifestyle. The Friend also preached that every being holds an inner light that is the living spirit of God. These beliefs were a mash-up of Quaker, Baptist, and other religious ideas that reflected the religious experimentation of the time, but because they came from the Friend, they seemed startlingly different and new.

New York, where the Friend eventually settled, was a natural place for religious experimentation because it had ratified freedom of religion as a state before the Constitution was written, and upstate New York became home to many experimental religious colonies, including that of the Universal Friends, just as it would later be home to hippie communes, lesbian separatists, and Radical Faerie communities. But throughout the existence of their ministry, the Friend's leadership was controversial. Because the Friend's detractors saw the Friend only as a woman rather than as the genderless person the Friend identified as, practices like the men who belonged to the Universal Friends doing chores led to accusations of their emasculation. Both male and female Universal Friends were allowed to preach and do ministry, which was almost unheard of at the time, and which created further scandal around the burgeoning religious community. And curiosity about the Friend's gender identity never went away, much as it doesn't for gender-nonconforming people today. When the Friend traveled to Philadelphia in 1782 to preach, outraged people asked for the Friend's gender, and the Friend replied, "There is nothing indecent or improper in my dress or appearance. I am not accountable to mortals. I am that I am."[6]

The Universal Friends' community, unfortunately, fell apart soon after they retreated to the land they lived on near the Finger Lakes. Legal disputes, hunger, and infighting caused tensions, and the Friend's health began to decline. By the time the Friend passed away in 1819, American Christianity was in the Second Great Awakening and becoming more emotive and expressive and less theological, much the same as it is today. Once the Friend died, the Universal Friends, who never numbered more than a few hundred, scattered. What's more, the Revolutionary War had prompted a growing American notion that men are the fighters and leaders of the nation, meaning that religious groups who weren't led by men would have a much more difficult time becoming established and gaining followers.

However, when the Friend was discovered by the internet late in 2019, the response was explosive. "This is the coolest fucker ever," wrote a Twitter user who'd posted a picture of the Friend and a link to their Wikipedia page.[7] The tweet had over a hundred thousand likes, and another Twitter user replied, "Christians: you're either male or female! Public Universal Friend: hold my Bible."[8] Shortly afterward, *the Washington Post* ran a feature story on the Friend,[9] and the NPR history podcast *Throughline* dedicated an episode to the Friend's story.[10] Two hundred and forty-four years after the Friend rose from a sickbed, America was finally ready for a gender-nonconforming religious prophet. But another one had also come along in the twentieth century, and America largely failed to notice when it happened.

———

Pauli Murray's life was a series of denials followed by resistances. This not only applied to Murray's race—as a Black American born in 1910, denial of Murray's worth was part and parcel of Murray's very existence—but it also applied to Murray's idea of gender, and to gender's limits on Murray's choices and experiences. In 1977 Murray was the first Black woman to be ordained in the Episcopal Church and, in 2012, was given a commemoration date on the Episcopal Church's sanctoral calendar—milestones achieved only after a lifetime of other milestones. Throughout life, Murray chafed against normative ideas about what was expected of women and about what womanhood meant.

Here the issue of pronouns gets complicated. Murray lived in a time before "they/them" pronouns were commonly used, and in journals and personal writing, Murray used "she" pronouns even while using them to talk about Murray's discomfort with gender. As a Black person who could sometimes pass for white, and as a person who internally identified as male even while experiencing sexism aimed at women, Murray's pronouns are an issue of identity from beyond the time in which Murray lived, even while Murray's experience of gender feels very familiar today.

"At times," writes Simon D. Elin Fisher, "Murray purposefully played with the norms that shifted as s/he moved across geographies and institutional settings, but s/he was acutely aware that the power to name her/his race and gender was rarely in her/his hands."[11] And Fisher notes that in Murray's case, the "s/he" pronoun is chosen because Murray moved from a masculine identification during his thirties and forties, to a stronger identification with female experience from her fifties until her death. "They," though commonplace today, is ahistorical, according to Fisher; trans and nonbinary clergy as well as Black female scholars I spoke with about Murray agreed. As a nonbinary friend noted, Murray's experiences could read as either transmasculine or nonbinary, but because Murray is the only person who could tell us what pronouns to use and is no longer living, that makes this differentiation difficult. My clergy friend also agreed that erasing "she," which was Murray's personal pronoun of choice, is problematic. As scholarship about gender-nonconforming people evolves, it's not unlikely we will eventually settle on a way to talk about pronoun use for those who have passed, but that moment has not yet arrived. So, going forward, I will use "she" for Murray while acknowledging that this is an imperfect choice, and that as a cis woman, I can only do my best to honor Murray's own struggles while hoping to respect her intentions and masculine identity as well as her external advocacy for women's rights.

At a young age Murray settled on a career as an attorney, after experiencing what she would later refer to as "Jane Crow," the overlapping of sexism and racism, long before the scholar Kimberlé Crenshaw coined the term "intersectional feminism" for a person's experience of oppression caused by overlapping institutional forces. In 1940, Murray and a friend had been arrested for sitting in the whites-only section of a bus, prompting Murray to go study law at Howard University. In these years, Murray was beginning to write in her journals about her discovery of people who were then called "pseudo-hermaphrodites," who felt they were a different gender from the one assigned to them at birth. Years before we even had a language for transgender people, Murray spent two decades searching for a doctor who would give her male hormones—and failing.

When Murray applied for postgraduate law study at Harvard, she was firmly told, "You are not of the sex entitled to be admitted to Harvard Law School." Murray shot back:

> Gentlemen, I would gladly change my sex to meet your requirements, but since the way to such change has not been revealed to me, I have no recourse but to appeal to you to change your minds on this subject. Are you to tell me that one is as difficult as the other?[12]

After Harvard rejected her, Murray did postgrad work at Berkeley, then lived for a time in Ghana before returning to America just as the women's movement was coming into national prominence. As Kathryn Schulz writes about Murray, who spent her entire life as a passionate advocate for women's rights, this letter to Harvard about changing her sex wasn't just making a point; it was "telling the truth."[13]

Murray privately identified, at that point, as a man. She wore pants, had short hair, and wrote extensively in her journals about feeling male. Her longest relationships were with women, but Murray rejected the idea of lesbianism—perhaps, according to Schulz, because of the cultural misunderstandings of lesbianism that existed at the time. After an early, failed marriage to a man, Murray believed the only reason she might be attracted to women was because she was, somehow, biologically male, and she went through batteries of medical tests to see if that was indeed the case. It was not, and eventually, Murray seemed to settle on identifying as a woman most of the time. But then late in her life, she also experienced a religious awakening that would yet again make her a pioneer.

As a civil rights attorney in a time when only a few Black women in America occupied those jobs, Murray experienced othering and sexism, common in that era. At the March on Washington, although many powerful women from the civil rights movement were in attendance, none of them was invited to speak: Ella Baker, Fannie Lou Hamer, and Rosa Parks, among others, were effectively silenced by leadership. Later, Murray would write that she hated being "fragmented into Negro at one time, woman at another, or worker at another,"[14] which happened to Murray over and over again. In spite of her achievements as an attorney and civil rights activist, the intersecting oppressions of racism and sexism meant that Murray struggled to make a living throughout her life, until she finally landed a tenured professorship at Brandeis University. Upending expectations, in her sixties Murray resigned from that position in order to become an Episcopal priest.

In an increasingly secular America, the fierce religious convictions of many civil rights leaders are often played down today. Clergy, however, played an important role in helping the movement define its notions of justice as well as find its nonviolent approach. The Rev. Dr. Martin Luther King Jr. was, of course, a minister first and doctor second, but in more recent years the "Dr." has sometimes overtaken the "Rev." For the women in the movement, faith was also a guide that helped shape their understanding of equality as a matter of moral urgency. Fannie Lou Hamer had deep religious convictions and described Christ as a revolutionary, Ella Baker helped found the Southern Christian Leadership Conference, and Pauli Murray's religious convictions guided her throughout her life.

Ordination for women, when Murray felt herself called to it, was not even a possibility in the Episcopal Church. "In classic Murray fashion," writes Schulz, "the position she sought was officially unavailable to her."[15] Murray enrolled at the General Theological Seminary in New York anyway, with good timing. In 1977, the Episcopal Church voted in its General Convention to ordain women, and Murray was ordained just a few days after that vote. She celebrated her first eucharist at the same church where her grandmother had been baptized, as a slave.

Just a few years later, Murray died.

Most of her life was lived behind the scenes, but as acceptance of gender-nonconforming people grew and access to her private papers became available revealing her struggles with gender identification, Murray became a singular figure for those digging into the intersections of religion, gender, and social justice. Even so, both the Public Universal Friend and Pauli Murray represent the kind of hidden life many gender-nonconforming people still live today.

As much as we are moving beyond gender in many ways—and as fruitful and interesting as the spaces between gender identities can be—complementarianism remains an entrenched concept in both religion and society, hemming men and women, cis and trans alike, into untenable positions between expectations and reality. When a non-binary person like the Friend or a masculine-identifying person like Murray is coded as a woman, even today that identity is hard to split off from the ideas people have about what a woman should be, even if that person is not, internally, a woman at all. And when we factor in religion and faith, a person taught that God made gender binary will have further layers of conflict to peel back.

Will we ever be able to stop defining one another from the outside in? That is the question many gender-nonconforming people have to wrestle with every single day. Policing whether or not a person is a "real" woman based on biology is yet another form of trying to control women, cis and trans alike. Rather than focusing on biological differences, women might consider why we identify ourselves in the ways that we do, and what commonalities exist between cis and trans women. Some of those commonalities are the dangers we face from men. The male fear of a trans woman not being "real" explains why violence against trans women occurs at higher rates than it does against cisgender women. According to the National Center for Transgender Equality, one in four trans people has faced a bias-driven assault, and those rates are even higher for trans women of color.[16] According to the advocacy group Rape and Incest National Network, for cisgender women, the rate of experiencing sexual harassment or violence is closer to one in six.[17] Both are unacceptable and call for cis and trans women to band together, as natural allies, rather than being pitted against one another in a competition for some kind of imagined authenticity.

However, for some feminists, this allyship has not been the case. TERFs, or trans-exclusionary radical feminists, were not something most people were aware of before 2020, when J. K. Rowling, the author of the Harry

Potter series, began expressing anti-trans views on social media, leading to a backlash from many of her younger fans, who had grown up with a broader understanding of gender. *TERF* has become a pejorative term, but the attitude that sex is solely biological is one that's been part of many feminist circles as well. Gender, for Rowling and others like her, cannot be separated from biology, and because a trans woman might not share the same biological makeup as a cis woman, the argument goes that she is therefore not a woman.

Among the problems with this argument, it doesn't make logical or even biological sense in providing definitions. Every cis woman who lives long enough to go through menopause will stop making estrogen in large enough quantities to qualify her as a biological woman. Not all women menstruate; not all women have breasts, ovaries, or uteruses; not all women bear biological children. So the argument that sex and gender are purely biological crumbles under examination. And gender-nonconformism has existed as long as gender has. There is evidence of it everywhere in history, around the world, and, as we've seen, in the beloved Middle Ages that Harry Potter books often take as referent.

Wilgefortis may not have been real, but what Wilgefortis represents—rebellion, stubbornness, defiance of authority, and freedom from the constraints of gender's expectations—is a very real story for many people throughout history. This is true for people of faith as well, and not just Christians. From the Native American Two-Spirit to the genderless and gender-shifting Buddhist bodhisattvas to the Muslim trickster djinns to gender-transforming Hindu deities to the hundreds of references to different gender identities in the Jewish Talmud, Wilgefortis is just one example of the ways in which the religious imagination is much more interesting than we might expect. Wilgefortis, after all, was renamed Uncumber and Liberata when she freed herself from expectations of gender. The real miracles happen in the in-between.

SIX

ANGRY

Dorothy Day was many things: a journalist for socialist and communist newspapers, a single mother, an adult convert to Catholicism, and the cofounder of the Catholic Worker Movement, a leaderless movement of volunteers living in radical solidarity with and in service to the poor and marginalized. She was a lifelong activist, tirelessly present at every protest, walking every picket line, repeatedly being arrested, spending long stints in prison, and participating in hunger strikes. She was deeply religious and saw her vocation as a call to solidarity with the outcast, without ever taking religious vows. She was also very, very angry.

She made other people angry, too. Most people saw housing the homeless as transitional, or as a form of rehab. But Catholic Worker houses are not rehab houses. They are homes. "We let them stay forever," Day once told a social worker. "They live with us, they die with us, and we give them a Christian burial. We pray for them after they are dead. Once they are taken in, they become members of the family. Or rather they always were members of the family."[1] She was no fan of capitalism or war, which made her a target for politicians, who distrusted her socialist background. And those who knew her intimately admitted she could be very difficult to live with: strict, demanding, impatient, and emotionally distant.

Scholars of Day have written that she "struggled" with her anger, that it was something she frequently needed to rein in. Catholic Worker Jim Forest, who knew Day in the last decades of her life, writes that her anger was something those around her experienced on a regular basis. When someone complained about her bad temper, she said, "I hold more temper in one minute than you will hold in your entire life."[2] When a college student asked Day about her soup recipe, she replied, "You cut the vegetables until your fingers bleed." She was angry at America, too, for its systemic failures to serve the poor and function with any kind of meaningful social equity. According to Day, "Our problems [as Americans] stem from our acceptance of this filthy, rotten system."

But she was also, by all accounts, a saint. She gave until there was nothing left, worked harder than anyone else, and was politically radical at the same time she was religiously conservative. Her days began and ended with prayer. She was someone who not only had religious convictions but actually lived them out, often at the expense of her personal life. She abandoned her common-law husband when she converted and he chose not to join her, but she also continued to write longing letters to him after they parted ways. She had deep wells of love for humanity that very few other people can approach, but she also knew that human beings can be frustratingly selfish and shortsighted.

She was a woman, and she was angry. All the time. Angry at injustice, angry at politicians, angry at people around her, angry at herself. Dorothy Day's anger might be dismissed as the same kind of "righteous anger" that has fueled prophets and leaders forever, but because she was part of a religious tradition where patriarchal thinking is so deeply entrenched as to be built into its foundations, her anger is often swept over in favor of focusing on her holiness. This not only does a disservice to Day, who famously said she didn't want to be called a saint because she didn't want to be "dismissed so easily," but it also does a disservice to women's anger, so threatening to men's grip on the status quo that they have spent millennia trying to tamp it down for fear of what might happen were it to be fully unleashed.

The dichotomy and problem of women's anger is that it is both universal and largely perceived as aberrant by patriarchal culture, and therefore something to be suppressed. Since Saint Paul—or whoever put his name to these texts—wrote them down, these words about women have had unfortunate consequences:

Women should be silent in the churches. For they are not permitted to speak, but should be subordinate, as the law also says. (1 Corinthians 14:34)

I permit no woman to teach or to have authority over a man; she is to keep silent. (1 Timothy 2:12)

These are just two examples of the kinds of silencing and erasure of women that formed the backbone of Christian patriarchy, but these ideas of submission and silence are still rolled out with some regularity today, not only by religious conservatives but by mansplainers, reply guys, and every other person who thinks they have more knowledge and more experience than a woman possibly could. When you're on the receiving end of it, there are a few common responses to this kind of thinking: corrosive self-doubt, lacerating irony, and incandescent rage.

Patriarchal culture that critiques women as being too emotional has somehow managed to erase the idea that anger is an emotion, because anger has become the domain of men. Rebecca Traister says that Americans in particular "are regularly fed and we regularly ingest cultural messages that suggest that women's rage is irrational, dangerous, or laughable."[3] During the Brett Kavanaugh confirmation hearings in 2018, the man at the center indulged in red-faced rage and shouting, and this was passed off as an appropriate response, an example of his "passionate" nature, his fervor for the law. When Christine Blasey Ford, who accused him of sexual assault, spoke calmly and clearly, using her expertise as a psychologist to support her points about trauma and memory, subsuming her anger and shame to professionalism and confidence in the truth of her narrative, she was attacked for not being "likable." Dr. Ford was not allowed the luxury of releasing her emotions on the public stage, even while she spoke about her own sexual trauma. However, holding back turned some people against her. This push and pull puts her and every other woman in an impossible bind. She got death threats and had to go into hiding. He got to sit on the Supreme Court. Surely she was angry about it.

The danger of an angry woman is the danger of insta-
bility, volatility. But a woman who holds in her emotions
somehow manages to fail as well.

In Greek mythology, the maenads were acolytes of
the god Dionysus, whom we now associate with booze
and parties. But the word *maenad* translates to "raving
one," and these women were both angry and dangerous,
an archetype and warning signal to men of what uncon-
trolled female rage can become. The maenads could not
be wounded in battle, and they suckled wolves instead
of human children. Snakes drank their sweat, and they
could uproot trees with their bare hands. They traveled
into the mountains at night and participated in violent
rituals, sometimes involving tearing a bull to pieces
with their bare hands and eating its raw flesh, ritualisti-
cally taking in the body and blood of Dionysus, a twist on
Christian communion with very different implications:
instead of imbibing peace, they imbibed fury.

There is a maenad inside every woman, still, today.

———

Every woman keeps a memory store of slights, abuse,
enforced subjugations within her: the times she was
undervalued, undermined, overlooked, and passed aside.
How were women taught to handle the fire inside? In
my Catholic-school girlhood, the model given for every
woman was the white marble statue of Mary parked in

a corner of the playground. This Mary was passive, an empty vessel created to hold God. We were given female saints who resembled Precious Moments figurines more than real people, saints praised for obedience and docility, unlike their male counterparts, who bravely spoke up and fought and shed blood for the Lord.

This was not the 1950s. This was the 1970s and 1980s in Oakland, California, a city defined by its radical activist history. While we were being taught that women saints never got angry, Angela Davis and Elaine Brown were carving out leadership positions in the Black Panther Party just a couple of miles away, clearly and appropriately venting their anger. While we were introduced to a Mary defined by submissiveness, who never spoke up, the ERA was being pushed along by women angrily shaking off their predetermined destinies. When we learned that women are not allowed to be leaders in our church, Shirley Chisholm was running for president, channeling her experiences of racism and misogyny into eloquent critiques of American oppression. While Pope John Paul II was writing that submission to men is how women experience love, we were watching the movie *9 to 5*, in which Dolly Parton, Lily Tomlin, and Jane Fonda's characters tie up and vanquish the horrible boss Fonda's character refers to as a "sexist, egotistical, lying, hypocritical bigot."

What the Catholic church wanted us to understand about women and anger—that we simply didn't experience it—backfired spectacularly. Gen Xers became, according to Pew Research, the least religious American generation up to that point, to be followed by the increasingly less religious generations of millennials and zoomers, each generation angrier than the next.[4] The tipping point was, of course, the election of Donald Trump, when hundreds of thousands of furious women poured into the streets around the world—maenads unleashed.

But patriarchy's last throttling grasp is strong. Women might be able to march, but we're also expected to placate and soothe—not ourselves, but others, and men in particular. And we're also told to be quiet, keep secrets, not tell anyone when we experience harassment or violence. And if we do speak, we are dismissed as "hysterical," exaggerators, liars, told whatever happened was "not that bad" or "not a big deal" or something to be moved past or pushed aside.

How are we not supposed to get angry about that?

In America, women's anger is not only sidelined but racialized and class stratified, with damaging, long-festering stereotypes of "angry" Black women and "fiery" Latina/x women portrayed in opposition to "submissive" Asian American women. For Black women, this patriarchal culture is exemplified by the "Sapphire" caricature, who has "venom for anyone who insults and disrespects her."[5] This racist caricature morphed into the "Sassy Mammy," brought to a wide audience through the *Amos and Andy* radio show—a loud, overbearing vision of Black women that remains persistent as a stereotype today. Likewise, the notion that Latina/x women are hotheaded and liable to pop off has been reinforced in popular culture for decades. The short stories and novels of the Dominican American writer Junot Díaz are full of these kinds of feisty female caricatures, and television shows and films are still regularly populated with these emotionally unpredictable stereotypes of Latina/x women as well.

Asian women, on the other hand, are victims of the "docility myth,"[6] exhibited in fetishizations of Asian women portrayed by white media in "an almost entirely sexual light," according to Robin Zheng.[7] Portrayals of angry white women are more recently mostly focused on "Karens," entitled types who vent their racism and rage by calling in managers and cops to police what they believe is other people's problematic behavior. These white women use their anger to ward off perceived danger, which is often greatly exaggerated, if not entirely invented. This may explain why 53 percent of them voted for Donald Trump in 2016.

Each of these stereotypes does the same thing: it reduces women's humanity and mutes the lived truths of their lives. It pushes anger down into a place where it festers and feeds on our bodies and minds.

In a country built on a mythical meritocracy that supposedly levels the playing field, women of color and women in poverty are doubly disadvantaged. They're disadvantaged because of their gender, and also because of their lack of social cachet. They're also often stereotyped as angry, when in fact, they are often carrying centuries of inherited trauma. Trauma, scientists have discovered, can actually alter a person's DNA. And one of the predominant ways trauma gets expressed is through anger. So women are not just carrying anger from this lifetime. It's actually built into our bones.

———

In 1906, the tectonic plates below the Pacific Ocean off the coast of San Francisco tilted, slipped, and ground into one another, destroying most of what was then a city of four hundred thousand people more than half of whom instantly became homeless as the city's wood buildings burned and the mortar in its brick buildings liquefied, turning a city built on dreams of gold into a pile of smoldering rubble. Three thousand or more people died, and those who survived streamed into Oakland and Berkeley across the Bay, moving into makeshift shelters and encampments, scattering across beaches and parks throughout the Bay Area.

In 1906, Dorothy Day was a girl of nine, living in Oakland with her family, who led an itinerant existence as they followed her father's career as a horse-racing reporter. They only lived in Oakland for a few years, and their timing was, arguably, terrible. The quake put a stop to horse racing and ended her father's career at the newspaper, but it also sent floods of refugees from San Francisco into the city where she lived. She had nightmares about the quake for the rest of her life, imagining "a great noise that became louder and louder and approached nearer and nearer to me until I woke up sweating with fear and shrieking for my mother."[8]

In her autobiography, *The Long Loneliness*, Day wrote that the quake began, as they so often do, late at night with an audible rumble, and that "the convulsions of the earth started afterward, so that the earth became a sea that rocked our house." Her family home was "cracked from the roof to the ground," with objects knocked over, but Oakland did not buckle as badly as San Francisco. In a self-revealing moment that she drops into the text before swiftly turning the focus to others, Day notes that her father and mother snatched her brothers and sister from their beds to stand protected in the doorway, but left Dorothy behind, where she lay terrified "in a big brass bed that rolled back and forth on a polished floor."[9]

Scholars of Day and many others who view her with a kind of reverence that she, in her deep-seated pragmatism, would probably have disliked have written about the quake and its aftermath as the incident that began her slow transformation into a life given over to service. Her mother and neighbors rushed into helping the refugees in Oakland, cooking, cleaning, giving away "every stitch of available clothes"[10]—an occasion she would remark on as showing her the potential for human generosity.

But as a fourth-generation Californian who has lived through many earthquakes, from tiny night shakers to the massive Loma Prieta quake in 1989 that took down the Bay Bridge and flattened a section of freeway not far from my own family's home, I think about nine-year-old Dorothy left behind in her bed in Oakland, rolling back and forth across the room. I consider the nightmares she'd have about the quake for the rest of her life, and I understand she was very likely suffering from internalized trauma. And trauma can make women very angry.

In 2008, a group of scientists discovered that children who had survived the Dutch Hunger Winter were more likely to have more health problems than their siblings who escaped it. As mentioned earlier, trauma can in fact alter your DNA, meaning that trauma can also be passed along to succeeding generations. Much of the research on epigenetics since then has focused on World War II and the Holocaust, and there is growing research into links between the history of slavery and inherited physical and mental health issues in Black Americans.

Of course, we have long been aware that trauma alters people psychologically, something women were reminded of again during the #MeToo movement when woman after woman talked about the mental and physical damages of abuse. But the idea that our DNA itself can be permanently changed by trauma is something those who have survived violence or abuse can understand intimately. We don't know if Dorothy Day's anger as an adult was a direct result of her childhood experience in the earthquake or of being left behind while it ravaged her home. We do know that she could be cantankerous, short-tempered, difficult, and emotionally distant. For people like her who have survived catastrophes, the vulnerability of childhood combined with early trauma can take the form of anger in adulthood.

When I was a college student, a friend gave me a copy of an anthology by the local avant-garde book publisher RE:SEARCH. It was called *Angry Women* and had a cover depiction of a rigid-faced Medusa. The book contained a variety of essays by performance artists, experimental musicians, and writers, all talking about the ways in which they channeled trauma and their ensuing anger about it into art, lived with anger, cultivated it, and made it part of their creative process. But in my early twenties, I was already learning that anger was a luxury. I had an angry father, and anger made him drink, and drinking killed him, so anger had to be carefully meted out in small doses, like a homeopathic remedy. If you channeled your anger into social-injustice causes, it felt more permissible; in the early 1990s, AIDS was already killing some of my friends, and it was fine to lace up my boots and march with ACT UP and shout about the Persian Gulf War and go to shows by the local all-women band Tribe 8 and scream and jump up and down with hundreds of other angry women.

But at work, in class, with boyfriends, and walking down the street, it was not okay to get angry. Guys I dated thought their job was to get angry on my behalf. Whenever I'd get close enough to a guy to tell him about a sexual assault I'd experienced, he'd say he wanted to punch, choke, or kill the man who did it, and I was supposed to appreciate this, to consider it an honorific—allowing him the anger that wasn't allowed me.

I worked in retail to pay my way through college and grad school, and while it was probably within the customer's rights to get angry at me when I made a small mistake, the reaction to these mistakes was often disproportionate to the scale of my error.

When men would tell me to smile, would "Well, actually . . ." me in class when my points were in fact correct, would grab my breasts and ass on public transit, would follow me home, or on one occasion, grab my wrists and twist them so hard, one was sprained because he "just wanted to talk," getting angry was both my appropriate response and a huge mistake: it only amplified and intensified men's anger, like upending a vat of gasoline onto an already raging fire. Better to soothe and mollify than to risk making things worse.

Where does it go, all of that women's anger? In the catechism of the Catholic church, we are told that when anger turns to wrath, it becomes a mortal sin, one that will follow you after your death, unforgivable and as much a marker on your soul as those epigenetic changes are in the ladder of your DNA. "If anger reaches the point of deliberate desire to kill or seriously wound a neighbor," the catechism says, "it is gravely against charity."[11] Women get angry enough to kill, but hardly at the same rates men do; street homicides are primarily male-on-male crimes, and domestic murders are overwhelmingly examples of men killing women. This doesn't mean women don't or can't murder people or feel wrath; the "deliberate desire to kill" doesn't necessarily have a gender. The act of killing, however, does.

But women are also "cute" when they're angry, "spunky" and "sparky" and every other adorable adjective you want to layer on in order to avoid the fact that women's anger is so swiftly dismissed that it never has the capacity to develop any consequences, to scare anyone into change. If women's anger were allowed to be frightening, that would also mean facing the realities of letting it be unleashed. Women's anger may have, as Rebecca Traister says, "the power to change the world."[12] But we have to admit that for most women, it has yet to be set free and channeled to any degree that is truly world-changing.

In her landmark book of feminist theology, *She Who Is*, Elizabeth Johnson tells us that "a passion that often accompanies action on behalf of justice is righteous wrath," the response to the violation of human beings. Women, including many women religious like Johnson, have been taught not only to suppress their anger but that their anger is "something to be avoided, not nice, even sinful."[13]

Sisters and women in the Catholic church are expected to feel angry on behalf of the poor and the marginalized, to feel the anger of the Psalms and of Jesus flipping tables in the temple. That's righteous anger. But what Johnson and other Catholic women regularly experience is being told to mute, deny, or move past their anger at the church itself. I can't count the number of Catholic women I know who have been fired or had books canceled, articles pulled, and speaking engagements called off when they dared to be publicly angry about misogyny and corruption in the institutional church. The is the Janus face that tells women to be angry on behalf of others, but to forgive and let go and move past their own histories of trauma and hurt.

Perhaps righteous anger in women is in some ways more acceptable. After all, caring for the oppressed and downtrodden is built into the foundational values of every world religion. But the real threat is the irrational, everyday kind of anger that boils up from hormones and misogyny and racism and body-policing and constantly being told that you are getting everything wrong: wearing the wrong bra size and washing your hair wrong and having the wrong kind of eyebrows and wearing the wrong jeans for your figure/age and wrongly assuming that those years and years of perfecting your "I'm not angry" face have actually worked, because every woman apparently has a "bitch face," and nothing turns a woman into a bitch faster than expressing her anger. And what is a bitch, after all, but a name for a female dog: bred and born to be brought to heel.

For women this anger is intertwined with our experiences of religion, particularly in this era when the failures and abuses perpetrated by religious leaders are regularly laid bare for the world to see. Throughout the Bible, it is trust in God that brings people to safety, that shepherds them away from danger, that escorts them out of this life with grace. But when churches you invest faith and trust in victimize the most vulnerable, anger seems like a perfectly logical response.

I became a journalist who sometimes writes about clergy abuse because I was also a victim of sexual abuse. Because I was a child when it first happened, the patterns of abuse of the young and of women in particular are glaringly obvious to me as patterns we have yet to break. Hundreds of years of silencing and cover-ups will never come to an end until we allow victims to be angry about what happened to them; until we stand before that anger, witness it, and allow it to change us. And this same story unfolds in so many churches, so many denominations, so many faiths. Sometimes I can channel my anger into empathy, and what enables me to keep doing the work is my capacity to share others' experiences of shame, humiliation, and pain. I have felt those things, too, and I have been angry that anyone has been made to feel that way.

But my anger has never changed anything on a large scale, in the long run. It has perhaps moved people to reexamine patterns of behavior, but institutionally? No. My devotion to Dorothy Day as a model for living a life of faith is not just the sense that she is a model of self-abnegation, of the kenotic self-emptying modeled for us in the life of Christ, but also in the sense that she was angry, and particularly angry on behalf of the vulnerable, and in that sense, angry on behalf of herself because she, too, was vulnerable, just a child, alone. Perhaps that kind of anger only changes one person at a time. Perhaps it shifts things in increments.

I understand women's vulnerabilities with a particular acuteness. When my female students tell me about being groped, dismissed, mansplained, date-raped, talked over, passed over, silenced, or erased, I know that anger. I have held it closely for fifty years, getting to know it with an intimacy that sometimes startles me. Yet the righteous anger I feel on behalf of other women, the poor, immigrants, queer people, everyone marginalized and trampled upon by this system has also fueled the best of my work. Has this kind of anger changed the world? No. But what if women's anger is something we still need to learn to listen to, and to actually hear? In the middle space between her speaking it and how we react, a thousand different things can occur. And maybe, one day, for one person or many, one of them will be change.

SEVEN

ALONE

"One for solitude, two for friendship, three for society." This is how Henry David Thoreau described the chairs he kept in his house on the edge of Walden Pond.[1] But seventy-one years before Thoreau began his experiment of living in the woods, a fifteen-year-old girl named Sarah Bishop was captured and raped by British soldiers during the Revolutionary War after they burned down her father's house, killing everyone inside. She either escaped from or was released by her captors, and deciding that "she dreaded no animal on earth but man," Bishop withdrew into the mountains outside of Salem, New York, and scratched out a life alone in a remote cave for at least two decades.[2]

Like many women of her time, Bishop was deeply religious, and it was rumored that she kept dresses at the home of a family in town so she could change into them and attend services at the Presbyterian church. But for the most part, unlike Thoreau, who often had visitors, she avoided any company whatsoever and lived in her cave with no furnishings. She was described as a kind of feral specter, wearing a "confused and shapeless mass of rags, patched together without any order, which obscured all human shape excepting her head, which was clothed with a luxuriancy of lank gray hair depending on every side as time had formed it, without any covering or ornament."[3]

This "nun of the mountain" inspired wild rumors, including one that she had domesticated local rattlesnakes and could send them into town to fetch her milk to drink, like one of the maenads from centuries before. But the reality of her life was far more squalid, a survival story whose arc moved from tragic beginnings to a tragic ending. She kept only a Bible for company and ran away from people who came to visit her. Instead of a cozy home like Thoreau's, she lived in an unfurnished cave. She was most likely suffering from traumatic dissociation, for as one witness reported, "she appeared to have no sense of solitude, no weariness at the slow lapse of days and months: night had no darkness, the tempest no terror, winter no desolation for her."[4] It was one of those winters that eventually killed her. She walked into a bog and her feet froze into the mud, and there she died, her corpse remaining in place until it was discovered in the springtime.

In Tom Stoppard's drama *Arcadia*,[5] the mystery of an estate's "ornamental hermit" is revealed to have its roots in romance rather than war and violence. Septimus Hodge, a friend of Lord Byron's, is tutor to the teenaged Thomasina Coverly, who turns out to be a mathematical genius, much like Byron's real-life daughter Ada Lovelace. But when Thomasina dies in a fire at the end of the play, it's revealed that Septimus becomes the estate's hermit, driven to solitude by his grief over their thwarted love. (It must be said that Thomasina is only thirteen when the play begins, a fact that may be historically accurate but lands poorly with some audiences today.)

Men becoming hermits when tragedy strikes is a romantic vision in Stoppard's play, with Septimus spending the rest of his life in solitude, trying to solve Thomasina's mathematical theories, and living out the consequences of their doomed relationship. Like Septimus and Thoreau and so many others, the male hermit in the Western imagination is a romantic figure, choosing solitude as a kind of endurance test, the exemplar of the same vision of mythical rugged individualism that fueled so many ideas about manifest destiny. The female hermit is, instead, a freak, an escapee, a victim, a mystery.

Becoming a hermit is, of course, an extreme form of solitude-seeking for people of any gender. But for women in particular, who are expected by cultural norms to find their fulfillment in caretaking, nurturing, and mothering, the rejection of these roles is a particularly radical act. Whether she does this by choice or is driven by circumstances, she is making a decision few people can understand. A woman alone is both a threat, in the sense that she is not dependent on men, and someone constantly threatened, primarily because of men.

While some women, like Sarah Bishop, are forced into solitude due to tragedy, for many others, solitude can be a way to find and claim her sense of self-agency. There's a difference, too, between single women, who can still choose to surround themselves with friends and family, and women who are solitaries, who instead make a deliberate decision to go it alone. These deliberate women who crave solitude are often considered selfish in the same way that women who don't have children are considered selfish; rejecting the role of caregiver-nurturer means someone is always going to be puzzled, frightened, or violently reactive to that quest for solitude. But with it comes a new sense of self-reliance, and a chance for redefinition far from the prying eyes of society.

Spinsterhood and singleness are still, in many ways, viewed as failings, even when they're conscious decisions. millennials are less likely to get married than any previous generation of women, but even Gen X and boomer women have stayed single at a rate of about 15–20 percent. Even as shame and stigmas around singleness begin to fade, partnered women who still desire solitude will struggle to feel that desire as acceptable or normal. Women who like solo travel spend hours reading articles to prepare for the level of aggression they'll face, depending on where they're going. A woman arriving alone at a restaurant will still be greeted with "Just you?" And I can't count the number of times I've gone to a movie alone for a couple of hours of escapism, only to have a man sitting far away move into the seat next to mine, uninvited.

Solitude is the conscious decision to reject other people's expectations of what a woman should be, and it's often assumed that the solitary is also lonely. But solitude and loneliness are not the same thing. Beyond plain introversion and liking the freedom of keeping one's own company lies a more complicated series of decisions, including turning away from social expectations that make solitude look like a compromise instead of a choice. In his essay "Going It Alone," Fenton Johnson writes that "the call to solitude is universal. It requires no cloister walls and no administrative bureaucracy, only the commitment to sit down and still ourselves to our particular aloneness."[6]

That kind of focused attention is ancient, and common to all religious traditions. The Buddha and Jesus were both, by this definition, solitaries, as was Mary Magdalene when she walked alone to the tomb to keep watch.

There is obvious kinship between the kind of religious seeking that leads to solitary contemplative practices like the slow, careful scripture reading of *Lectio divina* or the long silent sits of Buddhist meditation. This is the pursuit of what monastics call the Great Silence, the long hours when speech is eschewed to turn one's attention to the quiet that brings us closer to a state of heightened awareness of self and what surrounds us—the silence that can also be called God.

Not only silence, but creative work requires solitude. And writing, of all creative work, may require it most of all: the extended time needed to either silence the inner chatter or tune into it is a process that differs with every word we set down, like seeking a particularly obscure radio signal on the left side of the dial.

Among the writers who have pursued solitude, only a few have been women who kicked off social expectations and went it alone, probably because that same shame and suspicion of solitary women has to be coupled with the fact that women were not widely taught to read and write until fairly recently in history. Among the male writers who chose solitude, Fenton Johnson mentions Emily Dickinson, the "high priestess of solitude," as well as Eudora Welty, Flannery O'Connor, Dorothy Day, and Zora Neale Hurston. Hurston, who was married three times, might not fit our typical definition of a woman in pursuit of aloneness, but she was also a mystic attuned to signals that we can only hear clearly when we peel ourselves away from the expectations of crowds. In her autobiography, *Dust Tracks on a Road*, Hurston wrote that "under the spell of moonlight, music, flowers, or the cut and smell of good tweeds, I sometimes feel the divine urge for an hour, a day or maybe a week. Then it is gone and my interest returns to corn pone and mustard greens, or rubbing a paragraph with a soft cloth."[7]

When we talk about women writers and the quest for solitude, we also have to talk about Virginia Woolf's *A Room of One's Own*, mostly because of its still-relevant manifesto about fiction-writing requiring time to oneself.[8] But Woolf, for all of her arguments about the necessity for women writers to have the same right to solo working spaces as men, was also a social creature who thrived in the companionship of the Bloomsbury Group, worked among her coworkers at the Hogarth Press, spent a stint in a collectivist group of neo-pagans, had a long marriage to Leonard Woolf, and engaged in multiple sexual relationships with women throughout her marriage, including an enduring one with Vita Sackville-West. We also have to acknowledge that Woolf, although she, like many other women who write, suffered from childhood traumas, also grew up in an erudite, upper-middle-class family with servants, went to Cambridge, and never really struggled to get by. Woolf may have argued that women needed a room of their own, but in her time and ours, that room is only within the reach of a few of us.

Solitude should not be a luxury, but in many ways, it is. That room was much more accessible to Woolf than it was to someone like Hurston, the granddaughter of slaves whose first job was as a maid. Or to Dorothy Day, who sought solitude while living in the Catholic Workers' Maryhouse on New York's Lower East Side, where Day's vision of Christian anarchy included unlocked doors and a stream of people coming and going every day. It is harder for a single mother or a Black woman writer or any woman writer from the working class to seek solitude than it is for someone like Woolf, who after a crowded and difficult life finally sought the ultimate solitude of death.

Casting off the attention-seeking world that rewards those who best hold others' attention means you can only rely on yourself, and that requires a level of self-examination and self-deconstruction that can be harrowing. In the Carthusian order, the most solitary of monastic orders, in which monks and nuns live in solitary cells and only speak to one another once a week during communal walks in the wilderness, the desire for solitude that brings people to the monastery is often greater than their ability to handle it. In Nancy Klein Maguire's *An Infinity of Little Hours*, a profile of a group of men who join the Carthusians in the early 1960s, only one makes it to final vows. The rest peel off, one by one, starved for conversation, attention, the feeling of being lost in a crowd.[9]

But religious solitaries nonetheless remain mythical and compelling figures, even if there are fewer women among them. The hermits, mystics, visionaries, anchoresses, nuns, priestesses, contemplatives, and witches who choose to turn away from expectations can help guide us to the overwhelming power that thrums beneath the surface of our human interface. These women are powerful because they are countercultural, but powerful also because they were able to tap into a deep, vital connection to the world around them, which in many cases led to great creative and spiritual foment. For this, they would face centuries of misunderstanding, judgment, sickness, shunning, rape, torture, and death. But they would also be rewarded with visions, privacy, the freedom to live simply, and the radical experiment of creating each day of their lives.

———

A woman is walled into a small room, which is attached to the side of a church. In that room, there is not much she can do other than contemplate and pray. There are two small holes carved into the walls of her room. One faces the outside world, and people approach it to ask her for advice and prayers. Another faces inside, into the church. Through this window she can receive blessings and eucharist.

Until she dies, she will never leave this room. Its bricks were laid with her inside, to seal her in, an anchoress.

We don't know much about how she passes her days except for the writing she leaves behind. Wildly imaginative and sometimes hallucinatory, her recollection of the visions she had while ill, *Revelations of Divine Love*, will survive the medieval era as the oldest extant book written by a woman in English. We do not know her real name or how she came to be named for the church her cell was attached to and the city in which that church stood. We do not know why she chose that cell, except that women had very few choices about their lives in her era. To us, she is known as Julian of Norwich, a solitary seeker of God, living through medieval waves of sickness, plague, and fear.

Mysticism, broadly defined, is the transcendent experience of an encounter with God. Sometimes this takes the form of a vision. For other mystics, it is more akin to the "still, small voice," a moment of encounter with the ineffable that becomes transformational to their spiritual lives. But the mystic always requires solitude.

In the early church, the Desert Mothers and Fathers experienced mysticism through contemplation, the silent practice of meditation. These "Ammas and Abbas" also withdrew from society to put themselves through what my spiritual director sometimes refers to as an extended psychological experiment: What happens if a person devotes all their attention, longings, and waking hours not to the material world, but to God? In the *Apophtheg-mata Patrum*, the *Sayings of the Desert Fathers*, we are told that a hermit in the 300s said that contemplation requires only a few steps, but it must always be done alone. "Take care to be silent. Empty your mind. Attend to your meditation in the fear of God, whether you are resting or at work."[10]

Evagrius, one of the first monks to record the sayings of the Desert Fathers and later a Desert Father himself, told his followers that mysticism required a threefold practice of purgation, illumination, and unification. In layperson's terms, this means that to have an encounter with God, individuals must first empty themselves of distractions, then be open to enlightenment, and only then can they achieve that elusive oneness with God or window into eternity. As you can imagine, this means that solitude only expedites the path to freeing the mind.

It was historically difficult for women to pursue this kind of solitude for obvious reasons. Particularly in the early church, women who lived alone were rare, and there are fewer Desert Mothers than there are Desert Fathers. Anastasia the Patrician, who is venerated as a saint in the Orthodox church, was among those who paved the way for women solitaries like Julian. Anastasia, a young widow who moved into a monastery in the sixth century, was being romantically pursued by the emperor Justinian against her will, so she sought help from an elder monk so that she might continue living out her religious vocation alone. This monk disguised her as a man and hid her in a remote cave, where she remained, living a solitary life of prayer, until her death, when it was discovered she was not the eunuch Anastasius but Anastasia. Today, queer Christians celebrate Anastasia as one of the first trans saints, but it's also easy to imagine her fear that the emperor would not leave her alone in her pursuit of solitude. That internal quest is so frequently interrupted and denied by others' needs and demands that it is sometimes tempting to imagine a cave as a real place of sanctuary.

But one of the things we learn from Julian is that sometimes the experience of emptiness and silence in solitude comes from outside of us, not from within. Julian lived through several cycles of the plague, and at one point, wished herself sick so that she might identify with the suffering Christ. But in her sickness, she also had a vision of Christ that revealed to her that suffering is not necessarily the best path to oneness with God. In Julian's vision, Christ takes up our suffering and unites his own suffering with ours to give us freedom. Oneness with God in solitude is not about suffering itself, but about accepting that God is still present in our suffering.

In her vision of the world held in God's hands like a hazelnut, Julian explains that this understanding "lasts and ever shall, for God loves it."[11] This is why she is also able to repeatedly tell us that in spite of whatever we are living through, "all will be well." And understanding that even in solitude, we are still not in control is, in some ways, what unites us with Christ, which is what Julian eventually came to understand. "We need to fall," she tells us in the *Revelations*, "for if we did not fall, we would not know how weak and wretched we are of ourselves, nor should we know our Maker's marvelous love so fully."

These solitary mystical visions of Julian's can sound like madness to our modern ears, now that we have effective mental health treatments available. The pragmatic American bent toward explaining everything away means religious experiences can more easily be dismissed as momentary distractions or flights of fancy. The commodification of "mindfulness" into apps and corporate-speak means that contemplation and solitude, too, are something to be bought and sold rather than experienced, a treat for the overworked.

But the Anglo-Catholic Edwardian mystic Evelyn Underhill, a British pacifist who lived through both World Wars, and a solitude-seeker even in her own long marriage, tells us that mysticism experienced in troubled times is meant to be a lived experience, not one to be over-analyzed. "Where the philosopher guesses and argues," she writes, "the mystic lives and looks; and speaks, consequently, the disconcerting language of first-hand experience, not the neat dialectic of the schools."[12] This is vividly shown in Julian's *Revelations*, where the language she uses to convey the sufferings of Christ and her own suffering and illness is sometimes downright gory, but the language used to describe transcendence, love, and recovery is in its own manner equally vivid.

Julian tells us that in times of historical crisis, "deeds are done which appear so evil to us and people suffer such terrible evils that it does not seem as though any good will ever come of them." When we focus on that, "we cannot find peace in the blessed contemplation of God," whereas God is constantly nudging us back into feeling God's love. "Pay attention to this now, faithfully and confidently," God says to Julian, "and at the end of time you will truly see it in the fullness of joy."[13]

But Julian's life was likely not entirely solitary. Women who were drawn to the anchorhold found themselves "squarely in the center of village life," their cells becoming in some cases "a sort of bank, post office, school house, shop, and newspaper," according to Robert Hasenfratz in his introduction to the *Ancrene Wisse*,[14] a medieval rule of life for anchorites and anchoresses. It's clear that while Julian was alone much of the time, living alone yet still being in the middle of Norwich, she was not as alone as Anastasia the Patrician. And as word of Julian's wisdom spread, she frequently had visitors.

Julian was in fact so well known in her lifetime that Margery Kempe, a mystic living nearby who as the mother of fourteen had a very different set of problems to deal with, made a pilgrimage to Norwich to seek Julian's spiritual advice. In *The Book of Margery Kempe*, which she dictated to a scribe since she could not write, Kempe, who was known for being highly emotional and bursting into noisy and disruptive tears during Mass, reports that the solitary Julian told her, essentially, that tears and hysterics were just fine. "Settyth al yowr trust in God and feryth not the langage of the world," Julian said to Margery, "for the mor despyte, schame, and repref that ye have in the world the mor is yowr meryte in the sygth of God."[15] One might even say, based on this encounter, that introverts and extroverts have much to offer one another.

But also: Julian and Margery were both mothers. Margery's obvious fecundity is one kind of motherhood, the kind a religious medieval culture is accustomed to. Julian, on the other hand, may or may not have been a biological mother—scholars have debated this. Perhaps her child or children died in the plague. Perhaps she was widowed. As with the lives of so many women, we just don't know anything about them except for the things men decided were worth writing down. Or in the case of Julian, what she recorded, which, about her own life and history, was so minimal as to offer no further clarity.

But people in her era called her Mother Julian, and many still do today. A solitary mother living in an anchorhold is not the mother most of us imagine, but a mother she was nonetheless: to the mad, the seekers, the prayerful and pious and confused, to anyone who came to the window. It is perhaps this dichotomy of a solitary mother that enabled her to tell us that God, too, the solitary God and the God we meet in solitude, can be our mother, as well as that solitary named Jesus, who, Julian tells us, gives us our being, "and this is where His maternity starts."[16] And what is maternal love but the same self-emptying love so many solitaries have given the world? Jesus, who drew energy from crowds and surrounded himself with a scrap heap of human beings, also needed, desperately and often, to be alone. Perhaps that's why Julian followed him into the anchorhold. Perhaps that's also why she kept finding him there.

———

When any woman walks into surgery, she walks alone—on the arm of a nurse or a PA or an orderly, someone kind and soft-voiced and swathed in scrubs and surgical bonnets and booties. But you, the patient, the woman, alone, are the one who will lie down, be peeled back and gutted. You wake up alone, the recovery room rocking and tilting. You go home with someone—they won't release you alone—but you recover, mostly, alone. When your person goes back to work and to their private distractions, you start walking a little bit, every day, alone, in loops around your neighborhood. Some days you push it too far and have to take a bus home.

But each day you walk farther and farther. Eventually you go into the parks and the woods alone, no cell phone signal, no music being funneled into your ears, just your two feet and the distance they create between what people expect of you and the person you are. In the Renaissance, writers like Montaigne personified nature as a woman, and perhaps the fact that nature is untamable and unmanageable is part of why you enjoy moving through her expanses.

"Don't you worry?" say some of your friends, knowing women get raped and choked and stabbed when they're alone, but it's honestly more frightening walking through any big city, feeling the pressure of other people's bodies, their stress and worry clotting the air, than it is being alone in the woods, at the beach, moving up and down the golden hills of California, dotted with dusty old oaks. You don't run like the sleek and driven women zipping past you, because your knees object, but you discover that trudging suits you. So you trudge.

Once in a while you'll pass a man on the trail and move pepper spray into your front pocket, but once your uterus is gone you also gain substantial amounts of weight, and between that and the silver filaments snaking into your dark hair, you're basically a nonentity in the eyes of men. They nod and keep moving. So do you.

Like so many women, you've been broken open by sickness and depression and anxiety and meeting everyone's needs, and it's hard for other people to understand that your reaction is not to call on people to help you through that brokenness, but to go through it mostly alone. To bring yourself back together, and back into being. The kind of change you're feeling is a change that you can only figure out on your own. It is the change from being one kind of person—attractive enough, capable enough, good enough, smart enough—into a person whose tank empties far more easily than it did in the past. You have limits now, and they emphatically make themselves felt. But past those limits, you walk further and further. You get trekking poles and ugly thick-soled boots and abandon your fashionable teaching and public-speaking clothes for compression leggings and fleece. Maybe this is just the inevitability of age, the sloughing off of external markers of identity, trading in the person who wears gold hoop earrings and ankle boots and wide-leg trousers and tasteful makeup for the person stomping through mud and dust, putting her life back together step by step.

Six months after surgery, you strap on a forty-pound backpack, climb a small mountain, and shiver the night away in a tent, alone, as the temperature drops down to freezing. But you are alive, and eating instant oatmeal in the morning, watching the winter's first storm rolling in over the Pacific Ocean, steel-gray clouds fat with the first rain in ten months, you understand this: survival as a woman requires other people, but it also requires learning to be alone. This is what Mother Julian knew, and Anastasia the Patrician, the Buddhist and Christian nuns awake late at night; what Sarah Bishop knew, even while wrecked by her trauma; and what God, the most alone among all of us, knows.

And if you're a woman, people are never going to like it. It will not make sense. They will always want a woman to be nurturing, solicitous, ready to easily slip into whatever archetype their needs declare, ready to be there for whoever needs her, whatever their needs may be. Sure, one or two women will be permitted to write bestsellers about being alone, but the happy ending is always that they get married or become mothers or preferably both.

This is not the ending you're moving toward.

You're just going to keep walking alone until your ankles or knees or hips can't take it, at which point you might get into riding horses or donkeys or maybe by then we'll have robot hips and knees or robot donkeys, who knows. And maybe it's not walking at all—maybe it's riding a motorcycle or taking up painting or quitting a soul-killing job or leaving a disappointing partner or going back to school and starting all over again. The only thing that matters is that you know how to keep moving and you understand the value of solitude and the Great Silence to move you, beyond anyone's expectations and outside of the circle of demands. When you were young, people made you. As you got older, you made yourself, even if that self being built was broken by the expectations of others again and again.

Now, maybe it's time to put those pieces back together. You know how to love people, and how to be with them, but you also know how to sit for an hour watching a cloud bend, how to draw your solitude around you in crowds, how to say no, you do not want to share your table and no, you cannot sit next to me in this movie theater, on this plane, on this train, on this bus. You know how to tell the difference between loneliness and its longing for others, and longing for solitude's pitched and heightened awareness; how to become a person who moves beyond the space between what everyone else wants from you, and who you have actually become. And in this, you meet something like Mother Julian did: a self who can accompany you, who can be a companion. You meet a giving, a receiving, a grace.

POSTLUDE
The Defiant Middle: A Manifesto

It's folly to believe we will somehow stop creating impossible expectations for women to live up to. For all of the defiant women I've studied, written about, befriended, and grown up with, most of them have not been able to shift the stubbornly persistent ways in which we are hemmed in by false expectations about what women should be.

And for all of the ways in which we are reshaping our ideas about gender today and what it means in terms of how women should think, feel, look, and act, the fact remains that my own church and many others will still not ordain women, we still have not elected a woman president in America, and women around the world suffer from violence and persecution every single second, to degrees and at a scale it is frightening to think about. We easily become numb to statistics and numbers. We become tired from lifetimes of being told what to do or think, or how to feel or look, and we inherit the exhaustion of living with those expectations from our mothers and grandmothers, stretching generations back.

Sometimes I consider my maternal great-grandmother, who had fourteen children she raised alone on a rural ranch after her husband shot himself. And I wonder how any woman could have survived that and still raise kids who'd end up becoming teachers and lawyers, including my grandmother, kid #14, who would attend UC Berkeley. Or I consider my paternal grandmother, who never went to college, or my own mother, who has lived alone longer than she was married and had a successful teaching and administrative career even while raising five kids, or my spinster great-aunt for whom I'm named, or the shadowy great-great-grandmothers coughing in the bowels of coffin ships or wrapping guns in blankets to hand over to the IRA, or the even more shadowy women stretching further and further back, aching and bending to men's wills, focused mostly on staying alive amid poverty and sickness and violence, most of it brought on by the fault and power of men. Their female descendants will never know anything about their interior lives; if they could write, they didn't do much of it, and we'll never know if those traumas they lived through were the bad seeds that bloomed in us into life-choking vines of physical pain and mental illness.

But somehow, like women all over the world burdened by expectations and responsibilities, they survived. And thanks to them and their survival, women like me will be able to make more choices about our lives than they could ever have imagined. But for all they survived and all we are surviving, we still remain caught in the middle, between expectations of how we should live and our lived reality.

Perhaps our future survival means reconsidering how we react to those expectations, how we can resist internalizing them, and how we do and don't allow others to shape us and the way we understand the world. Perhaps our future means focusing on what we can learn from other women instead of defaulting to the expertise of men, and considering how we can adapt, and what we can reject.

As a person who writes about religion and faith (which are—emphatically—not the same thing), I find each a fragile framework for anyone to build a life around, apt to shatter at the slightest disappointment, and if you're a woman who cares about religion, you are apt to spend plenty of time being disappointed. This is why we need to find other women in that same framework, other women who keep choosing to see the frame of faith and religion differently, who step into the frame and take their place, who bend the frame to accommodate those who have been rejected or, sometimes, who burn it down and start again.

When Joan of Arc died on the pyre, the fire revealed the hypocrisy and cowardice of the men who killed her. When Mary Magdalene walked alone to the tomb, with each step she became the church. When Mother Julian was walled into the anchorhold, people still streamed to her, sometimes across great distances and in defiance of danger. When people told Pauli Murray that as a Black woman she could not be a lawyer or a priest or queer, she still found a way to be all of those things. To understand how women defy expectations, religion is not a bad place to start, but its history is also littered with the corpses of women who were the victims of religious men who damaged and killed women in the name of God.

But that God who damages and refuses to liberate is not the God most of us know. The metaphorical old white man with a long white beard has long proven himself useless to most of us. On a panel with a group of Catholic women a few years ago, I talked with them about our struggles with this version of God. Only one woman defended the patriarchal God, saying she needed that version of God to feel protected and safe.

But the writer of the Psalms tells us, "My soul [is] like a weaned child with its mother. My soul is like the weaned child that is with me" (Psalm 131:2). The God we meet is a motherly force, and a protective force, but motherly not necessarily in a biological sense: God also leads us to become our own mothers, which means giving birth to ourselves and re-creating ourselves, over and over again. That re-creation does not require male permission or institutional permission to envision God in any way that we want. When churches won't ordain us, we have to ordain ourselves.

Oftentimes that comes at a cost. Women have often been the ones to blow the whistle and hold the institution accountable when it comes to abuse, whether that abuse is physical, mental, financial, or spiritual. They've lost jobs and friends and influence as a result. They've been called liars and silenced by church authorities. But this, too, is the work of patriarchy and its nefarious offshoot, clericalism, which prizes the institution above the people working to salvage it. And as an institution, Christianity has long sought to define women in narrow and restrictive ways, but if women can begin to reject a narrow and restrictive image of God, perhaps one day we will also help create a less narrow view of ourselves and a less restrictive kind of church. Slowly but steadily, thanks to women, churches and religious institutions are being held to account for what they have done to women and men and children over the centuries, and *dum spiro spero*—when I breathe, I hope.

Perhaps that widening will manifest in secular spaces as well. Already there are signs of women choosing the people they will become instead of cleaving to prescriptive and stifling role-play. The shift from seeing powerful, wealthy white women as the center of feminism to a more horizontal and leaderless feminist culture, inclusive of people of all racial and social backgrounds and increasingly inclusive of trans and nonbinary people, is also crucial if we really want to remake the world. Just like religion, feminism must adapt and change—otherwise, it risks irrelevance in a world where it is more crucial than ever before to amplify and elevate the voices of all. We can learn to decolonize our minds from racism, homophobia, sexism, and patriarchy, which so often arrive hand in hand. And we *can* learn to undo outdated constructs of gender.

This doesn't mean sexism won't continue to shape our lives or determine the way people respond to us, but that we will insist on pointing it out when it happens so that it will happen, perhaps, less often. But again, this comes at a cost—and that cost is often women's mental and emotional well-being. The quest to change sexist ways of thinking can feel Sisyphean, a lifetime of teaching and explaining and pushing back.

And yet, we keep showing up, and we keep trying. And this is where it becomes clear that as much as a utopian vision of a world run by women is appealing as a fantasy, it is so distant from our lived reality that it will likely remain a fantasy for some time to come. So this is where we need to have some frank conversations, not just with men but with ourselves, and with other women.

We need to begin by saying: *We know that you (mostly) think women are worthy of respect and being treated with human dignity. If you do and say and think those things, it is probably because women have patiently and thoroughly explained to you, and to ourselves, over and over again, that we are human beings deserving of a fully lived existence.*

But we also know many of us still vote for men, support institutions run by men, go to churches run by men, pray to a male God, read more books by men than by women, watch sports played by men, and raise male children to accept their supposedly inherent social superiority.

Women theoretically participate in life as equals, but somehow, we are still always a little in the background, a little less likely to lead, express ourselves, speak up, survive life unscathed. And we watch younger women noticing the same things, still shaping themselves to a version of the world based on the idea that middle spaces between expectations and reality are places of deprivation rather than promise and discovery.

So we wait for anyone, including ourselves, to answer one question:

What are we going to *do*?

What are we going to do to stop forcing women to fit into expectations of what we should be?

We are here, together, waiting for an answer.

ACKNOWLEDGMENTS

Portions of this manuscript appeared, in different forms, in *America Magazine, Commonweal, The Revealer, Religion News Service,* Image Journal's *Good Letters* blog, and at the website of *On Being.*

Many thanks to everyone at Broadleaf, especially to Lil Copan for seeking this book out and helping to shape it, to Heidi Mann for sharp copy edits, Claire Vanden Branden, Marta Smith, the typesetters, cover designers, and everyone else involved. Thanks to my agent Michelle Brower for the long run and to Kate Mack at Aevitas Creative who also stepped in to help. I had the privilege of getting feedback on this book in progress from Stefanie Kalem and Elizabeth Costello, who are both brilliant writers themselves, and women with huge hearts. Thanks also to Jessica Mesman and Julia Walsh for being there to bounce ideas off of, along with everyone in my online writing communities, colleagues at UC Berkeley, and my students. Thanks to classmates and teachers in the spiritual direction program at JST and my goddaughter Laurel, along with Deborah, Jean, Dale, Nate, Sister Jean, Jason, Kyle, the late Fr. Al Moser, and everyone else who helps me with God stuff. I'm also grateful to the magazine

ACKNOWLEDGMENTS

editors who have helped shape my ideas. A good editor is like gold. Anyone who's been a friend, you are present in this book. Grateful also for the men in my life who get it, including Sam and Sage, and of course, for my mother, sisters, and brother, who have taught me life.

NOTES

PRELUDE

1   Gabriele Uhlein, ed., *Meditations with Hildegard of Bingen* (Rochester, VT: Bear, 1983).

2   Julian of Norwich, *Revelations of Divine Love* (Mineola, NY: Ixia, 2019).

ONE

1   Kyle McKinnon, "Will Malala's Influence Stretch to Europe?," DW News, January 18, 2013, http://www.dw.de/will-malalas-influence-stretch-to-europe/a-16532149.

2   Staff, *Transcript*: "Greta Thunberg's Speech at the U.N. Climate Action Summit," NPR, September 23, 2019, https://www.npr.org/2019/09/23/763452863/transcript-greta-thunbergs-speech-at-the-u-n-climate-action-summit.

3   Anatole France, *Life of Joan of Arc* (New York: Dodd, Mead, 1926).

4   Jessica Valenti, *The Purity Myth: How America's Obsession with Virginity Is Hurting Young Women* (Berkeley, CA: Seal Press, 2009), 13.

5   Diane Felmlee, Paulina Inara Rodis, and Amy Zhang, "Sexist Slurs: Reinforcing Feminine Stereotypes Online," *Sex Roles* 83 (2020): 16–28, https://doi.org/10.1007/s11199-019-01095-z.

6   "Child Pornography and Abuse Statistics," Thorn, accessed April 9, 2021, https://www.thorn.org/child-pornography-and-abuse-statistics/.

7   Sandi Villarreal, "Their Generation Was Shamed by Purity Culture. Here's What They're Building in Its Place," *Sojourners*,

accessed April 9, 2021, https://sojo.net/interactive/their
-generation-was-shamed-purity-culture-heres-what-theyre
-building-its-place.

TWO

1 Aretaeus, *De causis et signis acutorum morborum*, quoted in A Treatise on Hysteria, Robert Lee. J and A Churchill, London, 1871.

2 Laura Mallonee, "An Artist Takes an Unflinching Look at Her Own Hysterectomy," *Wired*, October 13, 2019, https://www.wired.com/story/elinor-carucci-midlife/.

3 Muhammad ibn Adam, "Do Women Have to Wear Hijab after Menopause—What about When They Are Elderly?," *Seekers Guidance*, November 3, 2016, https://seekersguidance.org/answers/hanafi-fiqh/women-wear-hijab-menopause-elderly/.

THREE

1 Simone Weil, *Gravity and Grace* (London: Routledge, 2004), 83.

2 Weil, 70.

3 Kim Jensen, "Fanny Howe" (interview), *Bomb*, January 1, 2013, https://bombmagazine.org/articles/fanny-howe/.

4 Gerard Manley Hopkins, *The Major Works*, ed. Catherine Phillips (Oxford: Oxford University Press, 2009).

5 Haley Byrd, "Ted Yoho Apologizes after Reportedly Verbally Accosting Ocasio-Cortez over Stance on Unemployment, Crime in New York," CNN, July 22, 2020, https://www.cnn.com/2020/07/21/politics/aoc-ted-yoho-confrontation/index.html.

6 Democritus Junior, *The Anatomy of Melancholy* (Project Gutenberg, 2004; updated 2021), https://www.gutenberg.org/files/10800/10800-h/10800-h.htm.

7 Paul R. Albert, "Why Is Depression More Prevalent in Women?," *Journal of Psychiatry & Neuroscience* 40, no. 4 (July 2015): 219-21, https://www.ncbi.nlm.nih.gov/pmc/articles/PMC4478054/.

8 Debbie Nathan, "What Happened to Sandra Bland?," *The Nation*, April 21, 2016, https://www.thenation.com/article/ archive/what-happened-to-sandra-bland/.

9 Sylvia Plath, "Lady Lazarus," in *Collected Poems*, Harper Perennial Modern Classics reprint ed. (New York: HarperCollins, 2018), 244–47.

FOUR

1 Rebecca Solnit, "The Mother of All Questions," *Harper's*, October 2015, https://harpers.org/archive/2015/10/the-mother-of -all-questions/.

2 Cynthia R. Chapman, "Barrenness," *Bible Odyssey*, https:// www.bibleodyssey.org/en/people/related-articles/barrenness.

3 Letty Cottin Pogrebin, "Miriam's Cup," The Shalom Center, accessed March 25, 2021, https://theshalomcenter.org/purim -to-pesach/miriams-cup.

FIVE

1 Darcey Steinke, *Flash Count Diary: Menopause and the Vindication of Natural Life* (New York: Farrar, Straus & Giroux, 2019).

2 Gina Hens-Piazza, "Silence Breakers: Woman Zion and the #MeToo Movement (Lamentations 2:20–22)," *WATERtalks: Feminist Conversations in Religion Series*, May 6, 2020, https:// www.waterwomensalliance.org/silence-breakers-with-gina -hens-piazza/?utm_source=rss&utm_medium=rss&utm _campaign=silence-breakers-with-gina-hens-piazza.

3 "Jefferson's Letter to the Danbury Baptists: The Final Letter, as Sent" (1802), *Library of Congress Information Bulletin 57*, no. 6 (June 1998), https://www.loc.gov/loc/lcib/9806/danpre .html.

4 "Chicago Clock; Universal Friends; War Dogs," *History Detectives Special Investigations*, Season 8, Episode 11, PBS, https:// www.pbs.org/opb/historydetectives/video/1579336059/.

5 "Public Universal Friend," *Throughline*, NPR, March 5, 2020, https://www.npr.org/transcripts/812092399.

6   "Public Universal Friend."

7   Commandersnacks, "this is the coolest fucker ever and an insp
     to everyone that wants a cool new name," Twitter, Decem-
     ber 7, 2019, https://twitter.com/commandersnacks/status/
     1203157015352102913?lang=en.

8   Holland (doilookpeng), "christians: you're either male or
     female! the public universal friend: hold my bible." Twitter,
     December 7, 2019, https://twitter.com/hubertvanwaddel/
     status/1203258656399282176.

9   Samantha Schmidt, "A Genderless Prophet Drew Hundreds of
     Followers Long before the Age of Nonbinary Pronouns," *Wash-
     ington Post*, January 5, 2020, https://www.washingtonpost
     .com/history/2020/01/05/long-before-theythem-pronouns
     -genderless-prophet-drew-hundreds-followers/.

10   "Public Universal Friend."

11   Simon Elin Fisher, "Pauli Murray's Peter Panic: Perspectives
     from the Margins of Gender and Race in Jim Crow America,"
     Transgender Studies Quarterly 3, no. 1–2 (May 2016): 95–103,
     https://www.academia.edu/29099709/Pauli_Murrays_Peter
     _Panic_Perspectives_from_the_Margins_of_Gender_and
     _Race_in_Jim_Crow_America.

12   Kathryn Schulz, "The Many Lives of Pauli Murray," *The
     New Yorker*, April 10, 2017, https://www.newyorker.com/
     magazine/2017/04/17/the-many-lives-of-pauli-murray.

13   Schulz.

14   Schulz.

15   Schulz.

16   "Anti-violence," National Center for Transgender Equality,
     accessed March 26, 2021, https://transequality.org/issues/
     anti-violence.

17   "Victims of Sexual Violence: Statistics," RAINN, accessed
     March 26, 2021, https://www.rainn.org/statistics/victims
     -sexual-violence.

SIX

1 Jim Forest, "Servant of God Dorothy Day," Catholic Worker Movement, accessed March 26, 2021, https://www.catholicworker.org/dorothyday/servant-of-god.html.

2 Jim Forest, "The Trouble with St. Dorothy," *U.S. Catholic*, November 1, 1997, https://uscatholic.org/articles/200807/the-trouble-with-saint-dorothy/.

3 Rebecca Traister, *Good and Mad: The Revolutionary Power of Women's Anger* (New York: Simon & Schuster, 2019), 25.

4 Pew Research Center, "Religion in America: U.S. Religious Data, Demographics and Statistics," Religion & Public Life Project, September 9, 2020, https://www.pewforum.org/religious-landscape-study/generational-cohort/.

5 David Pilgrim, "The Sapphire Caricature," The Jim Crow Museum of Racist Memorabilia, Ferris State University, 2012, https://www.ferris.edu/HTMLS/news/jimcrow/antiblack/sapphire.htm.

6 Christine Ro, "The Docility Myth Flattening Asian Women's Careers," BBC, August 16, 2020, https://www.bbc.com/worklife/article/20200807-the-docility-myth-flattening-asian-womens-careers.

7 Robin Zheng, "Why Yellow Fever Isn't Flattering: A Case against Racial Fetishes," *Journal of the American Philosophical Association* 2, no. 3 (Fall 2016): 400–419, doi:10.1017/apa.2016.25.

8 Dorothy Day, *The Long Loneliness: An Autobiography* (San Francisco: Harper & Row, 1981), 20.

9 Day, 21.

10 Day, 22.

11 *Catechism of the Catholic Church* (Vatican City: Libreria Editrice Vaticana, 2019), http://www.vatican.va/archive/ccc_css/archive/catechism/p3s2c2a5.htm#2302.

12 Traister, *Good and Mad*, 28.

13 Elizabeth A. Johnson, *She Who Is: The Mystery of God in Feminist Theological Discourse* (New York: Crossroad, 2002).

1 Henry David Thoreau, *Walden* (Boston: Houghton Mifflin, 1906), 155, https://www.walden.org/work/walden/.

2 Tim Abbott, "'Like a Ghost to Glide Away': Sarah Bishop, the Hermit of West Mountain," *Walking the Berkshires*, October 23, 2006, https://greensleeves.typepad.com/berkshires/2006/10/the_lonesome_de.html.

3 W. Beach, "Sarah Bishop: American Hermitess," *Sarah Bishop*, https://www.sarahbishop.org/about-sarah-bishop/about-sarah-bishop-2/.

4 Tim Abbott, "Recollections of Sarah Bishop," *Sarah Bishop*, https://www.sarahbishop.org/about-sarah-bishop/about/.

5 Tom Stoppard, *Arcadia: A Play* (New York: Grove, 2017).

6 Fenton Johnson, "Going It Alone," *Harper's*, April 2015, https://harpers.org/archive/2015/04/going-it-alone-2/.

7 Zora Neale Hurston, *Dust Tracks on a Road* (New York: HarperCollins, 1996), 213.

8 Virginia Woolf, *A Room of One's Own* (London: Hogarth, 1929).

9 Nancy Klein Maguire, *An Infinity of Little Hours: Five Young Men and Their Trial of Faith in the Western World's Most Austere Monastic Order* (New York: Public Affairs, 2006).

10 Jenn Strawbridge, "3rd and 4th Century Social Distancing in the Desert," *Theology*, accessed March 27, 2021, https://www.mansfield.ox.ac.uk/3rd-and-4th-century-social-distancing-desert-jenn-strawbridge-theology.

11 Julian, *Revelations of Divine Love*.

12 Evelyn Underhill, *Mysticism: A Study in the Nature and Development of Spiritual Consciousness* (Mineola, NY: Dover, 2002).

13 Julian, *Revelations of Divine Love*.

14 Robert Hasenfratz, *Ancrene Wisse* (Kalamazoo, MI: Medieval Institute, 2000).

15 Lynn Staley, ed., *The Book of Margery Kempe*, bk. 1, part 1, 1996, https://d.lib.rochester.edu/teams/text/staley-book-of-margery-kempe-book-i-part-i.

16 Julian, *Revelations of Divine Love*.